*"Cellebrating"*
# CellChurch Magazine

# "Cellebrating"
# CellChurch Magazine

Compiled by

## M. SCOTT BOREN

TOUCH PUBLICATIONS
Houston, Texas, U.S.A.

Published by TOUCH Publications
P.O. Box 19888
Houston, Texas, 77224-9888, U.S.A.
(281) 497-7901 • Fax (281) 497-0904

Cover design by Don Bleyl
Text design by Rick Chandler
Editing by Scott Boren

International Standard Book Number: 1-880828-21-9

TOUCH Publications is the book-publishing division
of TOUCH Outreach Ministries, a resource and
consulting ministry for churches with a vision for
cell-based local church structure.

For more information on other
TOUCH Publications or CellGroup Journal
Call 1-800-735-5865 or 281-497-7901.
Find us on the World Wide Web at
http://www.touchusa.org

# Contents

# Introduction

In 1992, I received my first copy of *CellChurch*. I must have read it cover to cover ten times or more. I was dreaming as I read it. I only wanted to find a cell church. Little did I know that I would one day edit and write for the magazine.

The story of my first encounter with *CellChurch Magazine* can be multiplied thousands of times. The impact of this little magazine has surpassed any of our dreams. I remember talking to a pastor from the Aleutian Islands off the coast of Alaska. He called to thank us for the magazine, saying that put his dreams for the church into words.

Countless people have shared that they were left sleepless after reading this magazine and other cell materials. Hearts beat for a church that embraces community, and finally they saw a way to do it.

While many longed for the vision of the cell church in the early nineties, many judged the cell church with skepticism. Some even asked if cells were some kind of cult. Today the radical, fringe voices are not the only ones praising cell groups. Christian Schwarz, in his research on church health in over 1000 churches, concludes, "If we were to identify any one principle as the 'most important' then without a doubt it would be the multiplication of small groups."

While many argue that cell groups are crucial — including Peter Wagner, Leonard Sweet, Rick Warren and George Barna — there is very little agreement on how groups should function. Most conclude that they should be one of the things the church does as a part of its programs. Small groups become one of the choices of the church. While this is a step in the right direction, a different kind of church is having a greater impact on the world.

After Dr. Neighbour discovered this "different kind of church" in Asia and Africa, he explained it to North America through the publication of *Where Do We Go From Here?* and *CellChurch Magazine*. He called it the cell church, where the cell group is not just a Bible study, but a place where Jesus shows up. He helped us see that cell groups are not a program to make churches successful. They are a place to call home, a place where every member is released into ministry.

Now the cell church phenomenon is not just an international movement. North America can say that it works here. Churches large and small have changed not only their structure, but they have also become places that release people into ministry.

Over the last nine years, *CellChurch Magazine* has sought to provide church leaders with inspiring and practical resources to promote the releasing every member into ministry. Since *CellChurch* is now called *Cell Group Journal*, we wanted to preserve the timeless pieces that will continue to inspire and inform the church.

The articles by Larry Kreider and Bill Beckham will help you cast vision and develop strategy. Those by Ralph Neighbour, Randall Neighbour and Jim Egli will give you practical tools for cell life. And those by David Cho and Larry Stockstill will take you back to the beginning of every movement of God, prayer. Also included is a new article by Joel Comiskey.

May these articles bless you as you walk in God's calling for the church.

— M. Scott Boren
Compiler

# Catching the Vision

# Section 1

# 1

## Where Do We Go From Here?

by Joel Comiskey

*Joel Cosmiskey currently serves as a missionary with the C&MA in Latin America. He holds the Ph.D. degree from Fuller Theological Seminary in Intercultural Studies. Along with leading cell seminars around the country, he forms an integral part of the pastoral team in a growing cell church in Quito Ecuador. Joel and his wife Celyce have three daughters.*

*Where Do We Go from Here?* penned ten years ago by Ralph Neighbour, rocked the church world and helped create the American cell church movement. Neighbour's book pinpointed the stagnate and programmatic state of the North American Church, while highlighting the close community and evangelistic growth in the cell church. Neighbour ignited a fuse that continues to explode today. As this book celebrates its tenth anniversary, we need to once again ask the questions: Where do we go from here?

Neighbour initially attracted a crowd of dissatisfied pioneers, much like David who gathered "All those who were in distress or in debt or discontented . . ." (1 Samuel 22:2). In those early days, the only viable cell church models came from overseas. North Americans pieced together models and principles that might work in North America, but for the most part, they were immersed in theory. Few, if any, viable cell churches existed in North America. Anti-cell church foes repeated mercilessly the refrain, "It might work overseas, but it just won't work here."

Polemics often consumed those early days. The cell church movement in North America was trying to establish itself among the competing small group philosophies that dotted the American landscape. Lots of discussion, for example, simmered around the difference between a pure cell church and the meta model. Again, theory, more than practice, characterized those times.

A different landscape is now evident in North America. North Americans, pragmatic by heritage, can now see several prominent cell churches that embody the earlier theory. What does this mean for the future of the cell church as we enter the new millennium?

## New Prominence

Bethany World Prayer Center has had an incredible impact on the North American cell church scene. Bethany World Prayer Center declares by its very existence that the cell church can work in the U.S. Since becoming a cell church, BWPC has grown from a respectable church of twenty-five ingrown "fellowship" groups to a dynamic church of 600 multiplying cell groups. And in just 7 years! Bethany World Prayer Center, with more than 8,000 Sunday worshippers and 2 million-dollar annual mission's budget, dispels the myth that "cell churches just don't work in America."

Interest in Bethany is obvious. Its annual cell church conference increases in attendance yearly, attracting more than 1500 pastors and key leaders. The attendance highlights the desire of church leaders to see a living, breathing cell church, rather than discuss what a cell church *ought to be.*

What people see at Bethany is a synthesis of the worldwide cell church wrapped into a unique package for Baton Rouge. BWPC, in other words, has excelled in stealing the best with pride. Larry Stockstill recognizes in his book, *The Cell Church,* the major influences that have shaped them:

- 1992 Neighbour's book *Where Do We Go From Here* (derived principles)
- 1993 visited Faith Community Baptist in Singapore (copied the cell office structure)
- 1993 visited Yoido Full Gospel Church in Seoul, Korea (understood care/growth structure)
- 1993 visited Elim Church in El Salvador (understood the importance of evangelism in cells)
- 1996 visited International Charismatic Mission in Colombia and adopted G-12 principles

I've highlighted BWPC here, but Bethany is not the only exciting cell church blossoming in the U.S. Other North American cell churches are reaching into the thousands. Space doesn't allow me to talk about the exciting things happening at the Door of

Hope, Church of the Nations, Cornerstone Church, Colonial Hills Baptist Church, Clearpoint Church, Long Reach Church of God, and others.

The fact that the cell church can work in the U.S. has given new impetus and prominence to the cell church scene in the U.S. Pastors who were afraid of joining an underground fringe movement are now emboldened to follow these prominent cell church models.

I'm not saying that the cell church movement is now mainstream. Far from it. I am saying that the cell church movement in North America is gaining momentum and more church leaders are asking the questions, "What is the essence of the cell church?" and "What are the practical steps to become a cell church?"

## From Fringe to Mainstream

Few mainstream groups promote cell church as a viable alternative for their churches. Take my own denomination, the Christian and Missionary Alliance. The C&MA has a growing number of cell churches and many more interested in the cell church model, but cell church is not promoted on a district or national level.

After a recent cell church seminar in Philadelphia, I met with a C&MA pastor in a nearby restaurant. We talked about the cell church philosophy and its integration into our denomination. "Our district doesn't understand the cell church model," he told me. "If key leaders have heard about it, the understanding is often muddled or wrong," he continued.

In Indianapolis I ate lunch with a rising star in the C&MA whose church plant grew to 700 people in just seven years. This young pastor, well known in C&MA circles, plans to build a multi-million dollar complex. His interest in the cell church was evident, but he had no desire to identify with a counter-culture revolution called *cell church*. He simply wanted something better than his current philosophy. "What is the essence of the cell church?" he asked me in a million different ways. "How can I best integrate what we're currently doing well with the cell church?" Do I need to get rid of *all* of my programs? I sensed sincerity and urgency in his voice.

Pastors like this one are recognizing the benefits of the cell church, yet they're not interested in adopting some of the counter-culture elements that they perceive in the cell church. They simply desire something that will help them do a better job than their present church structure permits.

What can we say to this new generation of leaders? How can we help more people see the blessing cell concepts can bring to God's church? One way is clearly communicate the heart of the cell church so that others will see its value and desire to join in.

## The Essence of the Cell Church

These conversations, along with my own wrestlings, have stirred me to piece together the essence of the cell church. I've attempted to break down the cell church philosophy into its simplest form, so churches will see a clear path to follow as well as recognizing the destination upon arrival. As far as I'm concerned, the following comprise the *Big Three* of the cell church core.

- Definition of a cell based on components
- A strong cell system that concentrates on the cell
- Senior pastor's total involvement in cell ministry

### Correct Definition of a Cell

This issue, more than any other, separates the cell church movement from the plethora of small group philosophies. In today's small group market, it's vogue to label any small group a cell. This might include Sunday school classes, prison ministry task groups, church boards, choir groups, usher groups, etc.

One of the key distinctions of the cell church movement is the purity of the small group. Cell churches highlight the components of a cell and refuse to call a cell everything that is small and a group. These components include: knowing God, knowing each other, and reaching out so that others know Jesus (with the goal of multiplication). Cell churches want to know that those attending a cell will experience community and have a chance to invite their non-Christian friends. Cell churches believe that labeling everything a small group will actually water down the cell philosophy.

My definition of a cell is: A group of people (4-15), who meet regularly for the purpose of spiritual edification and evangelistic outreach (with the goal of multiplication) and who are committed to participate in the functions of the local church.

My definition makes it clear that I am referring to church-based small groups. Those who attend the cell groups are expected to attend the church celebration. The goal of the cell is multiplication.

### A System That Concentrates on the Cell

Concentration — a positive term — must be our rallying cry. To succeed in cell ministry you must give it chance to fly. Concentration equals cell nourishment and long-term care and assures that cells will survive and flourish.

In a million different ways, church members must hear and see that the cell is the base of the church. They must unconsciously understand that success means leading a cell group. Concentrating on the cell church system stimulates church members to enter the equipping track with the goal of eventually leading a cell group. If your cell system, on the other hand, is one program among many, it will neither care for current cell leaders nor empower members to open new cell groups.

I've discovered that this is a tall order for many churches. I challenge these pastors with a positive message of integration, rather than a negative one of *ridding yourself of all filthy programs*. Integration involves intense planning to assimilate current programs into the cell church system (or let them die a natural death). Integration demands hard questions and honest answers. It takes time and energy, but the fruit is well worth the passing pain.

### The Senior Pastor's Total Involvement in Cell Ministry

At a Houston cell conference, an associate pastor approached me in despair saying, "Is it possible for our church to become a cell church, even though my senior pastor is juggling a dozen programs?" How I longed to offer him an encouraging word, but I lacked one. I said to him, "In all honesty, unless your senior pastor is leading the charge, you'll never become a cell church." This is a fact. Perhaps the clearest distinction between a church with cells and a cell church is the senior pastor's involvement. The senior pastor in a church with cells delegates the cell ministry to an underling, while in the cell church the senior pastor leads the charge.

Don't misunderstand me. An associate pastor or even a zealous church member can help the senior pastor catch the cell church vision. But until he does, the church has little chance of becoming a cell church.

In our cell church experiment, it took one year for the senior pastor to truly capture the cell church vision. When starting, he had a cell vision, but the vision didn't have him. It didn't possess and control him. It took its place in the long-line of high-powered programs. He didn't really understand the need to concentrate, nor promote the cell church vision before the congregation.

Those initial months were some of the hardest in my life, because I wasn't sure if he or the church was going to make it. I understood that unless he caught the vision, we'd stagnate as a church with cells.

The good news is that the cell church vision has captured the heart of my senior pastor, and we're now growing like wildfire (1997-21 cells; 1998-110 cells; 1999-250 cells; 2000 goal-400 cells). My prayer is that the same will be true in your church.

## Beyond the Big Three

Surely, there are other important aspects of the cell church: pastoral care system, leadership training, statistical follow-up, offices, etc. However, these additional aspects flesh-out the skeleton. The big three lay the foundation.

Any church that defines it's small groups accurately, concentrates on building a cell system, and is led by a senior pastor committed to the cell church vision has arrived at the ball park. To win the game, additional features must be added in the process, but at least the game can begin.

My concern is that we don't entangle the cell church movement with endless strings of cell legalism, for which everyone has a different set of standards. Let's proclaim the good news of the cell church to those starting churches or desiring a change. Let's keep our message simple, understandable and not make it so hard for people to join this wonderful movement.

## Cautions in the Cell Church Movement

As the cell church movement heads into the next millennium, we have a better chance of success if we take heed to certain precautions.

### The Language Barrier

It's time that we change our language in the cell movement. I'm afraid that at times we've created a negative image of *program haters* or *people against the traditional church*. This image helped create the movement and even sustained a core group of guerrilla warriors who wanted something that the program church could not offer. However, we're in a different time. Some of the most prominent churches in the U.S. are cell churches, and many others want to follow their lead. Let's begin with the good news, hold forth the benefits, and lay out the core principles (the big three).

### The Bunker Mentality

Several years ago, a C&MA church in Ecuador adopted one of the discipleship models on the market. This church wanted to make committed disciples of Jesus Christ that would eventually stir the church to grow. The mission gave this church a green light to run with their vision and even offered it our best missionaries and plenty of funds. When the mission inquired about the results, the answer was always, "We need more time. Discipleship is a long, drawn-out process. Eventually our church will explode, but we need more time." Ten years later, the church has yet to make a significant impact.

I've noticed this mentality on an ever-increasing scale in many *transitioning* cell churches. These churches have misinterpreted the purpose of the Prototype stage of cell development. They have seen the Prototype as the place where every detail about the cell group must be developed before they can move on. They work on the cell values so that the cell groups will eventually grow. But they have missed one point. They are not taking practical steps to grow the initial prototype group. They are not putting into practice the lifestyle that makes the cell grow.

I like to ask these churches: What are you doing right now to make your cell groups the central focus of your church? What are your cell multiplication goals for the next year? How are your cell church values manifested in an outward way? Do you promote the cell church vision constantly? Do your cell values stir you to create cell offices? How has your cell church values stirred you to reorganize your staff to be more compatible with the cell church?

Yes, change does take time, but we should never use that fact to excuse the lack of clear, urgent goals in the present. I call this the bunker mentality because these churches keep on adding *time* like a pain pill. It helps them live with the present, but does nothing to change their tomorrow.

Successful cell church leaders are intentional. They take clear, concrete steps to make their cell church experiment succeed. They're proactive, making history rather than becoming history. Starting with a quality prototype cell is only the beginning. They make clear, audaciously bold goals for the multiplication of cell groups. This requires intense leadership training and a clear focus on the cell system.

### Get Going

Experiences, not teaching, change values. Most of us have heard this many times. This phrase is commonly used to talk about equipping new leaders. Potential leaders must take incremental steps in leading a cell group before becoming cell leaders.

Yet sometimes we fail to apply this to the cell church transition. Church members will change when they experience cell life, see the positive results, and understand the cell vision because of constant promotion. I've noticed a tendency to ask church members to wait until they've reached a certain *value level* before allowing them to join a cell or become part of the cell church. On the contrary, churches and members transitioning to the cell church model will learn in the process.

## Conclusion

Where do we go from here? As we celebrate the tenth anniversary of this revolutionary book, we must peer into the next millennium with keen insight and added responsibility. We must build upon the theories of the cell church and work out what it means in real churches. We must take the principles and develop practices that work in specific situations

Recently Dr. Neighbour asked me for a definition of the cell church model in 10-15 words. I responded this way: "A New Testament movement that allows churches to experience unlimited qualitative and quantitative growth." I believe that the cell church is just that simple and exciting. As we share our excitement with church leaders eager to experience something better, I believe the excitement will grow as our cells produce fruit.

# 2

## Do Cells Really Work in America?
### by Larry Kreider

*Larry Kreider has pastored and also serves as the International Director of DOVE Christian Fellowship International (DCFI) for the past two decades. He has authored several books, including* House To House, *a practical manual for home cell group leaders including spiritual insights for the church of the 21st century. He and his wife, LaVerne, reside in Lititz, PA.*

One Saturday morning my daughter asked me to make her pancakes for breakfast. Knowing I am not a cook, I pleaded with her, "Please, Leticia, couldn't you just eat cereal today?" She persisted, so I tried. Half asleep, I read the instructions incorrectly, and the end product was horrifying! I asked her again to eat cereal. She persisted, and I tried again. This time the oil in the pan caught on fire! "Please try again, Daddy," my eight year old begged. I tried once more, this time without following the recipe on the side of the box. Amazingly enough, the concoction looked edible. Leticia took one bite of my freshly made pancake, looked up at me with her big blue eyes and said, "Daddy, may I have cereal, please?"

Likewise, we as a cell church had our share of mistakes. Our experiences were not unique. The lessons from these mistakes resonate in the hearts of pastors and leaders all over this country, yet there are those who give up just short of the lesson and leave with a bitter taste from errors. I once asked Dr. David Yonggi Cho, "Why is it, Dr. Cho, that it is so hard for cell ministry to work in America?" He responded immediately, "Many pastors are threatened. They are afraid to release their people." If this is why cell ministry hasn't worked in America, what can we do about it?

### The Control Factor

Rick Warren, the Senior Pastor of Saddleback Valley Community Church in Orange County, California, commented: "For your church to grow, both the pastor and the people must give up control.

The people must give up the control of the leadership, and the pastor must give up control of the ministry. Otherwise, either party can become a bottleneck for growth."

The traditional American pastor can control his church members, and the members can control the pastor. Pastors of cell churches are no exception to the control trap, and neither are cell leaders. In the beginnings of our cell church, we told people they must be involved in a cell group in their own community. This was a mistake.

One family felt misplaced in their community cell and came to me for assistance. I told them they needed to stay in the cell. As a result, they left our church. I recognized my mistake a few years later and asked them for forgiveness. I learned that the church is not built by geography, but by relationships.

Recently, I spoke at a church in upstate New York where the pastor had gone through a painful church split and decided to quit. However, the Lord spoke to him and said, "I have called you to release the ministry of the church to My people." That pastor returned to the congregation and began to transition the group into a cell church. When he released the people as ministers, the people released him and his leadership team to lead under the direction of the Holy Spirit. A fresh sense of faith and expectancy came into this church.

As believers mature and prepare to be sent out to start a new cell, many go back to their own neighborhoods. However, this time, they go back because the Lord called them there, not because of dictation from church leadership.

Dr. Cho warned, "Anything that destroys personal independence and the individual's personality and responsibility is from the devil. God never created us to be puppets. He gave us personalities to be developed into loving sons and daughters living in relationship with him. Our home cell groups are designed to promote that relationship." Cell groups can be used to either *control* God's people or to *release* God's people.

## Values or Methods

Why are values important? They are the core of our beliefs! They direct our actions and attitudes. Unfortunately, Americans often teach "methods" rather than Scriptural values. People become a part of a local church for the outward results but do not adopt the values of the church. When Christian leaders focus on methods rather than Scriptural values, the believer's belief system becomes based on the methods of men rather than on the Word of God.

For a season, our church spouted the cell church buzz words rather than testifying of Jesus and His Word. We exalted our cell vision above Jesus Christ. We prided ourselves in being the first cell church in our region! We soon learned that Jesus shares His glory with no other — no matter how great the cell group vision. We repented to the Lord and His people.

Soon after our cell church started, we traveled throughout the world to learn from others. When we returned from our first conference in Korea, we exhorted our cell leaders: "The Korean cell leaders multiply their cells every six months. We serve the same God. We expect you to do the same!" A few years later we repented to our cell group leaders for burning them out with a burden that was too heavy to carry. We taught a method rather than the Word of God.

Now, is it wrong for Korean Christians to have that goal? Not at all. Is it the Lord's will to multiply cell groups on a regular basis? Of course! Is it important to set goals? Yes, but we must understand from the Word of God why we should set goals and experience cell group multiplication. When we adopt other people's methods before understanding their values, we become frustrated and drained. People tire quickly of the latest Christian fad. They don't need it. We must fervently pray that our visions and goals are birthed by the Holy Spirit, not copied from the latest church appearing to be successful.

The American mindset focuses more on structure than on caring relationships and reaching the lost. Our methods must be the infrastructure that releases life. We must focus on life — not structure. If we are not careful, the results will be program-based cell churches. Focus on Jesus and His Word. Teach values first. Then apply the proper cell group structure.

## Consumers or Disciples

I was a guitar instructor a few years ago and met with students week after week, teaching them how to hold the pick, how to strum and how to play a certain chord. They practiced at home and came back the next week to learn another chord. Within a few months, they were playing dozens of songs. A cell leader disciples believers in a similar way. He or she trains the cell members by giving them responsibilities to help them grow spiritually.

Kevin was a young father in a cell group I led. One day he confided in me, "Larry, I have never prayed publicly. The thought of it really scares me, but I want to learn. I need your help. Sometime in a cell meeting, when I am not expecting it, ask me to pray." I assured him I would enjoy this opportunity! A few weeks later, at an early morning cell meeting, I looked in Kevin's direction and said, "Kevin, I would like you to pray this morning." He took a deep breath and prayed for the first time in public. It was his first step in discipleship. Kevin and his wife Carol became wonderful cell group leaders.

American Christians have swallowed the "holy man" and "holy building" myths. Every Sunday morning, they expect to find the holy man in a holy building who will minister to their needs. The holy man must be the counselor and must be available twenty four hours a day. Rather than becoming disciples and ministers, these well meaning Christians are merely consumers of ministry.

Pastors and their church members can develop co-dependent relationships. The pastor is paid to do the work of ministry; the people get their money's worth — good sermons and great programs. Inevitably, the pastor burns out, and the people never obtain the opportunity to fulfill their calling in Christ to equip and release ministers. They never become disciples.

The cell is only a forum to know one another, pray together and focus on reaching others for Christ. Real cell life happens after the meetings when believers share and pray together. This happens when believers practice hospitality in their homes and learn to know one another as real people. This also occurs when one believer assumes responsibility to help a younger Christian grow in his new life in Christ, meeting together each week for prayer, Bible studies and discuss questions about life. Real cell life comes when believers are either being discipled or discipling others. This forces consumers to become disciples.

## A Watered Down Vision

Too many times, after an American cell-based church grows and multiplies their cell groups, another migratory flock appears on the horizon. These are church people who see the new life in the cell-based church and want to connect with it. They leave their former church but bring in their former values and convictions. Immediately, the honeymoon wears off, and they long for the programs in their former churches. These consumer Christians voice their personal visions and perceptions of how the church must be run to the pastor and elders.

Gradually, church leaders walk in the fear of man rather than the fear of God, and they compromise the original vision the Lord gave them. Ministering in cell groups is minimized and replaced by new programs. The original vision for this cell church slowly ebbs.

At one point, our church was in this position. As a pastor, I reached the crossroads where I decided to continue with the Lord's vision, risking everything. I faced the possibility of having to start over with only me and my family. However, the Lord had graciously joined hundreds of sincere and dedicated people with us, and the risk did not result in complete loss. However, He needed to bring us to the place of willful obedience.

Over the years, we learned to ask God to bring us two types of co-laborers — new believers and those called to this house to house vision. Several times, we closed down our Sunday morning celebration meetings and met in homes for a month at a time. This helped people who were unsure of our vision to understand the importance of saints ministering from house to house. On one occasion, after we came back from a month of meeting solely in cell groups, we added one hundred people to the church. God places members in His body as He wills (I Corinthians 12:18), and misplaced believers experience much disappointment for themselves and their church leaders. At times, I have encouraged some misplaced people in our church to look for another church with a vision closer to theirs.

Earlier this year, as our church decentralized and became eight cell-based churches, I turned over the leadership and ministry of our cell church to eight pastors, twenty one elders and a host of cell leaders. I now have the privilege of being a pastor to pastors and training leaders in existing, newly birthed cell-based churches throughout the world. However, without believers trained in cell ministry, we could not make the transition.

## Forgetting Our Mandate To Reach the Lost

C.T. Studd, the famous missionary, once said, "I do not wish to live 'neath sound of church or chapel bell, I want to run a rescue shop within a yard of hell." The main purpose for every cell group must be to run "rescue shops," or the cell becomes a powerless social club. We are witnesses (Acts 1:8), not partakers of complacent, comfortable "bless-me" meetings.

Don and Jeanni served with a cell group in Harrisburg, PA. They believed the Lord birthed their cell to reach the lost. They hosted a Japanese student, Yosiko, enrolled in a local university. Week after week, they showed her God's love and prayed for Yosiko every week. A few days before Christmas, Yosiko, who grew up in a Buddhist family, declared to Don and Jeanni, "I have just received a Christmas gift. I have asked Jesus Christ to come into my life." The cell rejoiced with her, baptized her and discipled her. When the time came, they empowered her to go back to Japan. The entire cell was changed when they focused outward.

Americans tend to forget why they are involved in cell life. The primary purpose for the cell group is not merely for fellowship but to reach the lost. A cell group must focus on reaching people in and beyond their communities, or it becomes ingrown and stagnant.

Constant exhortation, encouragement and training from church leaders for our commission to reach the lost is vital. Without these things, the law of entropy occurs. Soon, the cell group loses its vision and mandate from the Lord to reach the lost. The tendency of all new wineskins is to get old, but bringing new people into the cell and multiplying keeps us fresh and alive.

The greatest catalyst for spiritual growth is getting our eyes off ourselves and on to Jesus Christ and His heart for the needs of those around us. Looking inward prevents growth, like an ingrown toenail, and usually causes pain, competition and stagnation. When groups are content to stay the same, they subconsciously build walls around themselves causing others to feel unwelcome.

## Lack of Desperation for God

I was recently asked to train cell leaders at the Vienna Christian Center in Vienna, Austria. Though only a few years old, it is the largest Protestant Church in the nation since the Reformation. It is a cell church, with cell groups scattered throughout the city. After speaking on "New Wine and New Wineskins," I opened the opportunity for prayer for these new leaders to receive more of the Lord's presence in their lives. One of the men, a diplomat, ran to the front of the room for prayer, desperate and hungry for more of God, and many more with the same desire followed suit.

Unlike much of America, there is a genuine hunger for God within believers in other nations. They believe that if God doesn't show up, it is all over! They are right! New wineskins (new cells) must be regularly filled with new wine (a fresh experience with Jesus). We must experience more of the life and presence of Jesus in our lives today than we did last week.

Americans trust structures rather than God. The Lord honors people who are desperate for more of Him in their lives. We cannot continue living on past experiences! We must be desperate for a daily and fresh touch from the Lord. We must expect the Lord to fill us with His presence when we come together in His name in our cell meetings.

Daniel and Rebecca Mbite, from Machakos, Kenya, started a new cell church last year. Daniel works for the bank during the day and serves as a pastor evenings and weekends. Rebecca gave up her job to have more time to minister to the needs of those they serve. They go into the villages and homes to pray for the sick, and the Lord heals them. Through these miracles, people give their lives to Christ and willingly open their homes for a new cell group.

A few months ago while I was in Africa, the cell church leaders told me Americans doubt there are demons in America. They doubt we believe in the supernatural world, because they know that demons are real. They grew up witnessing the supernatural through witch doctors in their villages, so they expect the Lord to work supernaturally among them in their cell groups.

In Acts 2, we see the early Christians empowered by the Holy Spirit to be ministers. Then in Acts 4, we see the disciples filled with Holy Spirit again! American believers need the same hunger for more of the Holy Spirit's presence and power. The church in America must experience a new desperation for God. We must believe in the supernatural. We must refuse to turn back, confess our mistakes and expect the Lord to help us into a new reformation.

Thousands of churches in America are presently transitioning into a New Testament model of Basic Christian Community. Saints are released to minister from house to house. To persevere, we must keep our eyes on God and His vision. There is no turning back! He wants to use you to fulfill His purposes. Jesus Christ will build His church, and the gates of hell will not prevail against it!

Perhaps you tasted and experienced cell ministry and became disillusioned or weary. Don't go back! Like I did with the pancakes, you may have read some of the instructions wrong or even neglected to read them. We must learn from our mistakes! The only people who never make mistakes are those who do nothing.

# 3

## Gentlemen, To Your Cars!
### The Eight Working Parts of a Successful Cell Church
by Bill Beckham

*Bill Beckham is the President of TOUCH Global, which ministers to churches internationally by establishing indigenous cell church movements within countries. He is the author of The Second Reformation.*

Those who come into contact with the cell church often feel that it is complex, confusing and painfully difficult to actually implement. The general consensus about the cell church is promising and exciting, but much too complicated!

Books, conferences and case studies on the cell church often add to the impression that we are looking at a extremely complex system. By the time all the different parts of the cell church are defined and described, the whole idea seems even more disjointed and involved.

Although our first impression of the cell church may entail ideas of great complexity, when properly viewed the cell church is a very simple and practical way of seeing the church. It is a correct theory, and "there is nothing so practical as a correct theory."

There are three factors that may contribute to the perceived complexity of the cell church:

- Approaching it from a mechanical rather than a functional perspective.
- Trying to use old operational procedures to make it work.
- Failing to distinguish between essential and nonessentials.

In order to experience cell church simplicity, you must see it in its functional rather than mechanical context. The functional context concerns itself with actually doing it — operating it. The mechanical context considers all the details about how all the parts of the cell church works. When we do this, we get bogged down in understanding the intricate details and often miss actually doing it. Consider the automobile. It is a "correct theory." If it were not a correct theory, we would not have cars all over the world causing traffic jams and pollution as the price of quickly getting from point A to point B. Like the cell church, the car is a practical and simple machine in its operational context but extremely complex in the mechanical context.

Suppose you are going to teach a man to drive who has never seen a car before. You sit him down in a small library of mechanic's manuals to explain how a car works. What will happen? As you begin to detail all the car's working parts, as laid out in the mechanic's manuals — the electrical system, transmission, engine and etc. — a spirit of complexity will take charge. The poor fellow will quickly reach the conclusion that he can't drive that car. "This machine is far too complicated to operate."

However, take that same person, seat him behind the wheel of the same car that looked so complicated in the mechanic's manuals, teach him about the steering wheel, the gas pedal, the brakes and the gear shift. Show him how to turn on the car, and he will learn how to drive. Remember, the car is "a practical theory" that functions simply at the point of operation. This is the primary point of understanding for one that wants to go from point A to point B. No matter how complicated the operation of a car may appear when one sits at a table with the mechanic's manuals, it is simple to operate from behind the steering wheel. In fact, most any person will be able to tell the key points about driving after an hour or two of practice.

Books, conferences and case studies on the cell church are often more like a study of the mechanic's manuals than instructions on how to operate the thing. Some select persons may need to know about the mechanical parts of the cell church and the automobile. However, aren't you glad that every driver isn't required to understand the mechanical intricacies of a car before being able to use it?

Fortunately, God has not assigned most of us to do the repair work on His Church, but to use it. If I am going to use a cell church, I need the simple instructions on how to operate the thing first, not the complicated procedures about how all the parts fit together or work. In fact, learning the simple operating procedures will then substantially increase my understanding of the mechanical details. I must see the cell church in its operational rather than functional aspect.

Using old operational procedures can also cause the cell church to appear complex. When new machinery comes on the market, often we need to unlearn old operating patterns in order to correctly operate the new machinery. Mixing new methods of operation with old ones can complicate the process and make a new, simple piece of machinery appear extremely complex.

My paternal Grandfather, whose life's stories have turned into great family folklore, had an experience that illustrates this principle.

One piece of folklore records the first time my Grandfather tried to drive a car. Since Pa, my Grandfather, was born in 1877, he came into contact with the automobile as a man who had already developed skills with other machinery. His primary experience was with farm machinery, pulled staring at the backsides of his two faithful mules, George and T Bo.

T Bo and George were operated with bits and reins and with voice commands: *gee* for right and *haw* for left; *get up* for start; and *whoa* for stop. Some operators of mules might have used more graphic commands, but as a serious Christian, Pa's working vocabulary was limited to these more acceptable, less colorful terms.

The first time Pa got behind the wheel of a Model A Ford, it ran away with him. The Ford was making right and left turns as if it had a mind of its own. He frantically tried to control the mechanical beast and bring it to a stop. In the midst of all the confusion, Pa reverted to his old way of operating machinery, which meant George and T Bo. He was heard desperately yelling, "Gee! Haw!" to give right and left commands. As the Model A headed toward an immovable object, he shouted, "Whoa! T Bo!"

Of course, the Model A tuned a deaf ear to such commands and would not respond to the same kind of operating procedures as George and T Bo. (From what I hear, George and T Bo didn't respond correctly every time either.)

I know my Grandfather survived that experience because he lived to be almost 96. But you know, I never did see my Grandfather drive a car all the time I knew him. Maybe he had already stopped driving by that time. Or maybe that one experience with the Model A Ford affected his attitude about driving cars and convinced him that the automobile was too complicated a machine to drive. Pa's bad experience was the result of mixing old operating procedures with a new kind of machine.

Even simple operations become complex if we try to use old operating procedures. Pa did not just need to learn how to drive the new contraption. Pa needed to unlearn how he had always operated machinery that was pulled by George and T Bo. His voice commands may have been designed for George and T Bo but not for Model A.

What does this have to do with the cell church? Old traditional operating procedures will not carry over in operating the cell church. Combining cell church operating procedures and those of the traditional church will cause confusion and complications. If you see the cell church as complex, it may be because you are mixing the old operating procedures you have used in the traditional church with those necessary for the cell church. This will surely bring confusion and doubt.

Failure to distinguish between essential and nonessentials will also cause the cell church to appear complex. The KISS principle comes into play here. "Keep it simple, stupid." Don't let the non-essentials that cause complexity confuse the simple and practical essentials that cause the cell church to work.

I inherited a 1984 Buick LeSabre from my Mother. It was a wonderful car in its day, offering every possible option known to man. Ron, my mechanic, loves that car. Every time I take it in for repairs, he assures me that my 1984 Buick LeSabre is special among cars built during that year. I often wonder something as I'm paying my monthly repair bill to him. Does his high opinion of my Buick have anything to do with the fact that he gets to repair all the fancy extras on the thing?

Now, my Buick would work with far fewer moving parts, the essentials — which are still doing surprisingly well. Its the nonessentials that are self-destructing. Don't get me wrong! All the fancy nonessentials are nice and do serve the important function of making at least one person on earth very happy — my mechanic. If a power window (which could be a simple handle) sticks in the down position, my mechanic gets to repair this non-essential luxury for a charge of $200. In the long-run, I would be better off if that 1984 Buick had fewer bells and whistles.

A cell church with minimum but essential working parts provides easy instructions for operation and low maintenance. These are the moving parts of the cell church. Get it right at these points and it will work. If we focus on these areas we need not be a rocket scientists to lead a cell church.

I want to put you in the driver's seat of a cell church and give you eight simple operating instructions. You don't need to be a trained professional to drive it — only one who desire to move forward. It is a correct theory (God's theory) and practical at the operating level. Give attention to these eight aspects of the cell church and it will work.

"Gentlemen, To your cars." Get your head out of the mechanic's manuals and get behind the steering wheel! Here are your instructions:

- Get into the CELL body of the car.
  The cell is the framework around which all of the parts of the cell church are fitted.
- Turn on the VISION key.
  Vision activates the cell church. Vision is the electrical system of the cell church.
- Put your hands on the LEADERSHIP steering wheel.
  Leadership guides the cell church.
- Fasten your SCRIPTURE seat belts.
  The Bible protects and provides safety for the journey.
- Activate the EQUIPPING gear shift.
  Equipping transfers the power from the driver to the engine.
- Make sure the EVANGELISM wheels are aired up.
  Evangelism takes the car forward into new territory.
- Check the WORSHIP gauge for fuel and water.
  Worship fuels and waters the life of the cell church.
- Let the PRAYER engine provide power.
  Prayer is the engine that furnishes the power of the cell church.

A car consists of hundreds of working parts. However, a relatively small number of its components cause the car to perform the primary function of moving from one place to another. For instance, if the transmission goes out, the car will just sit there even if all the other hundreds of parts are working. Likewise, a cell church has essential working parts that must operate before the cell church will work. Therefore, we must give our attention to installing the essential moving parts of the cell church.

The cell unit is the frame that integrates every other part of the cell church. As each car has a basic form that gives it identity, so the cell gives the cell church its identity. If it does not work here, at its most basic level, then the cell church will not work at all. The basic life of the church exists in the cell. The cell itself acts as the primary unit around which the entire church centers. Without this priority, the cell will become just another attached program, not the integrating element of cell church life.

Priority must be given to the dynamics of cell life and not just the mechanics. Make Christ the DNA of cell life: the life source, force and power. Focus the cell meeting upon Christ, not on techniques, leaders, materials or gimmicks.

- Acknowledge His incarnate presence
- Experience His omnipotent power
- Fulfill His Kingdom purpose

Group dynamics, effective leaders, celebration events, evangelistic campaigns, meeting mechanics, warm community or spiritual experiences will not sustain and drive the growth of God's work in the world today. Only a cell that allows Christ to actually move in the midst of the group can be His instrument in the 21st Century for "turning the world upside down."

Vision turns on the cell Church like an ignition switch starts a car. Vision creates the electricity that ignites the rest of the body. From my own experience, I describe vision as a call, a passion, a commitment, or even an obsession. If a church's vision does not work properly, everything will shut down, and the cell church will end up beside the road waiting for a tow truck. Leaders are responsible for clearly communicating God's cell church vision. A leader in a church outside of Washington D.C. shared this word: "When the vision is unclear, the cost is always too high." An unclear vision will result in a cost that proves too high, and the church will inevitably waver from the original call. Only a clearly communicated cell church vision will keep a cell church moving. Maintenance of an unclear vision will always become too costly. When this happens the leadership or the people will abandon the effort.

On the flip side, "When the vision is CLEAR, the cost is never too high." A clear cell church vision furnishes the necessary power and commitment to work till the end against all obstacles.

The leadership structure steers the work of the cell church. Just as we have a steering mechanism that directs the car, so does the cell church. Most cell churches follow Jethro's advice to Moses and develop workable leadership units through which God can direct

the movement of the church. Generally cell church leadership is arranged into the following four categories:
- Coordinating Leaders of congregations
- Area Pastors of 6-25 Cells
- Coaches of 3-5 Cells
- Cell Leaders of 5-15 Christians

This kind of leadership structure, integrated around the cell, allows Ephesians 4:11-12 to operate."And He gave some as apostles, and some prophets, and some evangelists, and some pastors and teachers to equip the saints for the work of service, to the building up of the body of Christ." When leadership works properly, Ephesians 4:16 begins to work. "The whole body being fitted and held together by that which every joint supplies, according to the proper working of each individual part, causes the growth of the body for the building up of itself in love." Servant leadership provides a way that primary care can take place closest to the primary need. At long last, Ephesians 4:12 can operate the way God designed it in the New Testament. God gives leaders to His church in order that He can steer the church in the proper direction. The cell church will simply not operate unless these leadership units are in place.

The Bible anchors and protects every aspect of the cell church like seat belts do passengers. Because the graded Sunday School is not the primary program in the cell church, some claim the cell church is a dangerous model without adequate biblical safety features. In actuality, the cell church releases the Bible to become part of every aspect of Christian life. The traditional way of doing Bible Study is not enough for the cell church. Many who have sat in our Sunday School classes, "hearing" the word for thirty years, can not even pray in public. They have not been taught to be "doers" of the Word. The traditional church's teaching of the Written Word has limited its application to cognitive understanding and little life transformation. However, in the cell church, members study the Bible in a way that teaches not only "hearing" the word, but "doing" the word. In the cell church setting, Bible Study is a lifestyle seven days of the week, not a study on just one day. In the cell church we find:
- Christ, the Living Word applies the Written Word through cell life.
- Every member is equipped in a systematic self-study of Scripture.

- The I Corinthians 14:26 pattern (everyone has a hymn, word, psalm, etc.) operates.
- The Word is read, sung and shared during worship times.
- Gifted teachers & preachers share the Word.
- The Word is consulted for planning and problem solving in all leadership meetings.
- Members are prepared to apply the Bible daily to their lives.
- Pastors, church planters and missionaries receive special equipping in the Bible.
- Youth & children learn to be "hearers" and "doers" of the Word in this pattern.

The Bible acts as the safety system that protects those traveling in the cell church from both doctrinal error and program deadness.

Every member enters a specific gear to receive equipping and then shifts on to the next gear of training. The cell church will not operate properly unless an effective Equipping Track exists so that each member is discipled and becomes "part of the solution rather than part of the problem." The equipping track systematically raises up healthy Christians who can move into the role of cell interns. Without cell interns, the cells cannot produce leaders, will not grow and cannot multiply. A cell church must set up a system of equipping gears that prepares each person for ministry at full-speed. General areas of training that seem to be common in such systematic equipping tracks are:

- Scripture foundation
- Christian values
- Kingdom living
- Witness
- Prayer
- Worship
- Cell Life
- Spiritual Warfare

Cell church equipping has three unique features: self-study, with a sponsor, and in a cell context. Equipping done through self-study proves most effective in teaching a new Christian "how to fish" rather than "giving him a fish." Through self-study with a sponsor, each cell member will enter into an accountable relationship with another person in the cell. Also, on the job training within the context of cell life accelerates the personal growth through each gear of training. The cell church will not operate without an effective equipping system.

Evangelism moves the church forward into the lost world. There must be something inherent within the nature of the cell itself that will overflow out into the world in witness. The higher a cell enters into worship in Christ's transcendent presence and the deeper a cell enters into community in Christ's immanent presence, the broader the cell will go out in witness and ministry in Christ's kingdom presence.

This car will not move without the wheels of evangelism. The cell provides the delivery system of the gospel out in the world, and is the church out beyond the parking lot. The cell offers a way that the church can become an exponentially multiplying force out in the world.

The lost are contacted out from the cell at three points:

- *We know them.* We know our *oikos* where relationship evangelism takes place.
- *They come to us.* Seekers and "men of peace" come to us.
- *We go to them.* We directly contact them at the point of their felt needs.

Evangelism in a cell church is incarnation evangelism. We drive forward to meet the lost instead of just inviting them to come to us. God established this model for evangelism when He left the comfort and glory of heaven to go into a lost world to seek and save that which was lost. The cell must not become just another "come structure," where we invite the lost to come to us. God has designed the cell as the ultimate "go structure," in which Christ continues to penetrate the kingdoms of this world by using each person in the cell.

Worship fuels the body with energy that flows from the presence of the Lord. In worship, the cell church experiences God both as the Most High God (Celebration) and as the Most Nigh God (Cell). God expresses Himself as the transcendent God and as the immanent God, the great God and the close God. Within the large and small group dimensions of the cell church, true celebration worship fuels and waters the life of the Church.

Worship takes place in several contexts in the full blown cell church:

- Family worship . . . Parent and children worship
- Cell worship . . . Small group worship

- Congregational worship . . . Extended family reunion type worship
- Celebration worship . . . Public event worship

As the life of Christ in the midst flows out of the cells, dynamic and meaningful celebration worship will naturally overflow into the life of the larger corporate body. Celebration worship will then flow back into the cells, fueling their life and ministry at the basic cell level. The old kind of Sunday worship operates out of balance and will hinder the movement of a cell church. Dynamic worship in every cell church context must exist if it will work properly.

Prayer is the engine that empowers the church to move forward in His work. Jesus said: "I will build my church . . ." Our part in Christ building His church takes place through prayer and communication with the Builder. Because the cell church will not work without Christ building it, the cell church depends totally upon prayer. The cell church must continually come back to the presence of God in order for the church to work.

Prayer in a cell church focuses on both the personal and corporate encounters with God in His greatness and closeness, in His transcendence and immanence. Between these two ways that God expresses Himself to His church there develops a flow of prayer. The more we experience Christ in our midst, the more we appreciate the glory and greatness of God in His transcendence.

Prayer takes on a new meaning in a cell church. Prayer during cell meetings. Prayer in leadership meetings. Prayer in the body life of the cells. Prayer in the "whole" church. Prayer in the family. Prayer as individuals. The cell church prays because it experiences the incarnation expression of the Most High and Most Nigh God. The cell church prays because it experiences what it means to be the Body of Christ on earth. Without prayer this car cannot move. The pistons that empower the cell church are only turned over through prayer.

Is the cell church simple or complex? It depends on how each one of us assembles it. Certainly God did not make it to be complex! If God has called us to be part of a cell church, He will provide a simple form of operation. Our success with the cell church does not depend upon our knowledge or expertise. (Even those early church leaders were considered novices.) If we try to understand every part of it mechanically, then it will look complex. If we let God put us in the drivers seat and operate the cell church, it becomes simple.

There is nothing so practical as a correct theory. The cell church is a "correct theory" because it is God's theory. Let's allow it to work in its simplicity and power by getting out of the library and into the driver's seat.

# 4

## Missions:
### Down-Shifting into a New Great Commission Paradigm
by Mike Cegielski

*Mike Cegielski is a cell-based church planter in Russia.*

Does your missions view need an overhaul to go along with your second reformation-style church? Here's one practical plan of action for cross-cultural cell missions.

"If it doesn't look broken, don't mess with it." If you agree with this philosophy, put this magazine down. I understand completely if your are overwhelmed with the transition your church is making to cells — just do faith missions as you have been doing all along. Find a missionary, support him, let him preach on Sunday when he visits, buy his kids new clothes and be a blessing to him! Faith missions have been the most successful worldwide evangelistic tool for almost two hundred years, and its success will not stop suddenly.

"If if jams, force it; if it breaks, it needed replacing anyway." Does this *Tim Allen* approach better describe you? Then join me in a practical look at a plan to fulfill the Great Commission with "more power" than current trends in missions.

Imagine this scene. My wife calls me from a pay phone from the local grocery store during a spring rainstorm. She informs me that the car has a flat tire and she needs a strong man to help a lady in distress. Desiring to stay dry and finish watching the ball game, I send my strapping young son to change the tire.

Who is the hero? Me, or my rain-drenched lad? The 16 year old who got the extra piece of pie at dinner will give you the correct answer!

Get the point?

While honoring the incredible job faith mission organizations have done in the past, we must step out into the storm and take local responsibility for world evangelism. When cell churches have "equipped the saints," they are going to be jammed with leaders ready to answer the call of missions. Will your church have a dynamic plan to support them in true second reformation fashion?

## Why Shift To Cell Missions?

### Indulgences and Committees

When the church begins to feel guilty because it chose a building program over a church planting program, a Christian ocean cruise over a short-term missions project or a new computer network over missions training, they call in the *missions friar*. He shows up and sells missions indulgences. Forgiveness for all their mission sin is offered at a fracture of what it would have cost to plant their own cross-cultural church. He tells them they have made a pleasing sacrifice unto the Lord — even though no one but a grandmother on welfare had to give up a dinner for their donation.

My wife and I were some of the first missionaries sent out from cell churches. We wanted deep relationships with the cell members in our supporting churches. Instead, we built walls called *committees* which managed our well-being. These dedicated folks quickly separated us from community with our fellow believers. The better the committee, the more we felt alone and disjointed from the body.

Then we thought, "If everything is supposed to be done in the cells, why can't we do missions in the cells? Our cell groups should be participating with the church planting teams which they support!"

Now that I have your undivided attention, let's discuss a new plan of action.

### Three Changes, and You're There

To effectively reach unreached people groups and start national churches, we have to redesign the missions structure. After five years of missions under church leaders, I see three changes cell churches must make from a church planter's view.

The first change is *responsibility and accountability* — who is accountable to God for the church plant? Second, *resources and opportunities* — who is to provide the training and resources to send the missionary out? And finally, *relationship* — who is to maintain the missionary in body life? With radical shifts in these three areas, a cell church will be able to effectively and efficiently plant cross-cultural cell churches.

When a church decides to support mission organizations and not plant its own cross-cultural churches, is it passing on the responsibility God has given it? Who is ultimately responsible for ensuring success or extra money for medical supplies? With an average of twenty-nine supporters, a missionary feels like everyone is responsible and no one is truly accountable. It's easier to defer to God's grace, give the missionary a few dollars and tell him, "Jesus will meet your needs."

Where is your church? If a member of your church comes to you stating God has called him into cross-cultural work, could you offer him an opportunity to become a missionary? Would you send him off to a missions organization with a symbolic $200 a month, hoping they could do something with him? With cross-cultural, cell-based missions, you could tell him you've been praying for missionaries to be raised up in the church and you already have a plan to train and send them.

When a missions program is delegated to a missions committee, relationships fade and a program is left as a remnant. If missions are rooted at cell level, a grass-roots commitment to the missionary will flourish. I found when I had "professional" relationships with pastors or leaders in a supporting church, they were not personally driven to communicate with me. In stark contrast, my cell leader and the two cells in which I fellowshipped pursued a relationship with my wife and I even though we never formalized their support of us on the mission field.

### What a Deal!

A shift to cell-based missions will allow you to take back responsibility. You can train up your own people and send them out to places where the Lord is calling your church to plant a new work. Finally, you can have meaningful relationships with missionaries on the field because you have a deep, established foundation. Get the picture? The cell church can become fertile soil for growing its own missionaries and planting cross-cultural churches.

## Moving Into Cell Missions

### One Church, One Baptism, One Mission at a Time

I understood cell missions at 4 years of age. My mom said, "You have to put that toy away before you can play with another." The reality of cell missions will come from a deliberate choice to do one thing well instead of jumping from project to project.

Make a strategy to plant one cross-cultural cell church and see it through. Your vision will be so specific that some members may not like its rigidness, especially those who have been called elsewhere. The church doesn't *support* missions, it *is* a mission! The vision to plant a cross-cultural cell church in a particular region will replace a policy that designates missionary support.

The strategic goal of cell missions is not just to plant a church in the 10-40 window, but to become a church mobilized for missions. How? By forming two training tracks — one for individuals to become missionaries and one to train the church at large. They are launched in tandem and are insufferably codependant. That's why it works.

## Making a Missionary

The secret to cell churches is that everyone is really being trained to be a missionary! Whether for a season or a lifetime, the principles and practices of the cell are culturally-acceptable worldwide; that means anyone trained in a cell church has a place on the mission field. Imagine the potential! Along with your church's standard training track from cell intern to zone pastor, a few additional requirements should be added to make someone missions-mobile. The training should be available to all members so a large pool of qualified people exists when missions needs and opportunities arise. Here's the process by which someone could rise in the ranks from cell member to cell church missionary. (I refer to the cell member as "he" only for the sake of writing simplicity. With fields "white for harvest", men *and* women must be trained for the task!)

### Candidate Missionary

This person thinks he might be called to be a missionary, or at least he wants some missions awareness. To become a recognized *candidate* missionary, he must complete the church's requirements as a cell intern, and take a short missions course (such as the Perspectives video course, Moody Missions correspondence course, or Emmaus Road's 3-day Intro to Missions in Tijuana). On the practical side, the student should go on a 2-6 week cross-cultural trip, preferably to a cell church. Finally, they would have to be an *assistant sponsor* for one the the church's missionaries, communicating and supporting them from the home base.

### Apprentice Missionary

The person seeking to become an *apprentice* missionary will have fulfilled the requirements for candidate missionary and have operated as a cell leader with one successful multiplication. His previous experience in missions will have confirmed a deeper calling into cross-cultural work. Upon confirmation, your church will prepare him as their future missionary.

To become an apprentice missionary, the person must complete a second missions course and attend a one or two week course on cross-cultural missions. On the practical side, he would spend two-four months helping a cross-cultural cell church, and be a *missionary sponsor* for six months, helping cell groups take care of their missionary. By the time a person was a qualified apprentice missionary, your church leaders must be willing to *fully support* the person to plant cross-cultural cell churches, as part of a team project.

### Missionary

A person would qualify as a fully-trained missionary after he had attended a twelve-week missions course like Emmaus Road ACTS 29 course, spent two-three years on the field in a cross-cultural cell church, and studied one-year equivalent of a foreign language and have achieved conversational fluency.

### Senior Missionary

A senior missionary will have completed all your church's training for a zone pastor. He would also have a BA, MA, or certificate in missiology. He would be fluent in a second language, and have spent four years in cross-cultural church planting, and have successfully planted a cell church in a different culture. This senior missionary is qualified to take teams out on the field.

As your church adopts this missionary training track and teams up for church plant projects, you might send out your missionaries under *other* churches' senior missionaries. The vision, however, would be that a church would eventually have its own fully-trained missionaries and teams on the field.

This type of training program also allows a church to raise up its own missionaries without a major burden on the church or the potential missionary. During his training, the future missionary grows deep in relationship with your church. However, to successfully move into cell missions, your whole church must make the missions paradigm shift and commit their resources accordingly.

## Mobilizing Cells Into Missions

For the new or small transitioning cell church (2-30 cells), the mobilization process will take about six years, unless trained people already reside in the church and are ready to be sent out. The three phases to missions-mobilization are: preparation, leadership development, and team projects.

## Preparation

In this first phase, your church must develop a missions training track, restructure the missions budget, and select an on-going cross-cultural work in which to participate. After one of your leaders or your pastor visits a potential mission site, an invitation is put forth to begin training for upcoming missions projects. Your potential missionaries are put into training and prepared to go. Meanwhile, your traditional missions committee is dissolved and a plan is written to phase out all random missions support over the next two years. As a substitute for the missions committee, a *missions mobilizer* is selected who will help a group of 3-5 cells participate in cross-cultural church planting. When the field site is selected, the field missionary will coordinate the sending of short-term workers, plans are arranged with the field missionary to send 2-3 short-term teams during the next two to four years. The group of cells also make plans to send their potential long-term missionaries for 3 month terms. During this two year period of partnership with a missionary on the field, your missions fervor will grow as most of your church has participated in helping the new church plant. Now your church is ready to move into the next phase.

## Leadership Development

During the two years your church works with a missionary, you should be looking for a new church plant location and for other cell churches who want to team up. From your cells' experiences on the field, look for the person who has risen up and is ready to go out as your first missionary. It will take almost all the church's resources to send out the missionary. Your cells have planned pastoral visits, short-term missionaries, and prayer and worship teams.

This team project has been planned for four years, and during that time many people will have the opportunity to gain experience in missions. The short-term teams sent out will become the foundation for a team project later. At the end of the four year project your church must raise up one senior missionary, one or two trained missionaries, along with many apprentices and candidates. Meanwhile, your membership has grown in confidence and understanding of cross-cultural cell church planting. You are now ready to plant another church!

### Team Projects

Six years have passed and your ten cells have grown to 40 cells in four districts. Each district is prepared to sponsor one of the four team members on your church plant team — a senior missionary, a missionary, and two apprentices. A younger cell church asks to send their first missionary out with your team for mentoring, and you readily agree. A missions organization has provided the cover to get your team in place, as well as contacts to help the team get established.

In time, your church will plant an indigenous church, but more so, you will have a fully-mobilized cell church in operation back in America. This process to missions mobilization demands great and focused commitment.

In the Preparation phase, your church sent out short-term teams to help one mission. Next, in the Leadership Development phase, the primary emphasis is on a single missionary. Finally, in Team Projects, the church is sending out groups of people to plant one church. Disciplined execution of the vision has allowed the cell church to become *fully* mobilized.

### Can It Really Happen?

This three-tiered plan will take commitment and effort to achieve success. Your church must develop the more practical parts of this plan, but the key is changing to cells planting cells instead of church supporting mission organizations. A group of committed cells will be needed to hold the missions "reins" and keep the buggy on the road. They will take ownership of the missions vision and patiently ride it out, avoiding rabbit trails and side trips. You can become a missions mobilized cell church!

## Accepting The Call

I have an Australian Shepherd named Shadow. As a puppy, she would instinctively try to herd things — cats, kids, tennis balls, with no idea what she was doing — it was just instinctive play for her. Unfortunately, I didn't have the ability or desire to train Shadow to use her God-given ability to shepherd other animals.

We have a whole pack of "missions puppies" in our cells who have the instincts for missions but need training. God wants to use them to fulfill His Great Commission. Unfortunately, most of them are running in circles, chasing their tails when it comes to missions.

Most churches have no serious desire or ability to mobilize their people into cross-cultural missions. Now is the time to accept our responsibility to evangelize our generation worldwide! When we look to closure of the Great Commission, it becomes clear that the Church has yet to mobilize itself. A new model for missions is needed to help churches mobilize; traditional missions structures fall short.

The traditional policy of churches supporting mission organizations is very limiting. Rather, we should mobilize our cell groups through a tightly-focused plan like the one describes here because it *optimizes the raising up of a church's own missionaries.* May your cell group boldly go to the "edge" where no Christian has gone before and bring Jesus to a dying world!

# Where to Begin

# Section 2

# 5

## The Ten Commandments
## of Transitioning
by Jim Egli

*Jim Egli and his wife Vicki serve as Small Group Pastors at the Champaign (IL) Vineyard overseeing a growing system of over 50 cell groups and target groups. He serves as a Trainer and Curriculum Consultant with TOUCH spearheading the Encounter God initiative. Jim is also the Director of Research for Missions International. He is completing a Ph.D. in Communication at Regent University. He and his wife Vicki have three young adult sons and a nine-year old daughter.*

Have you caught the cell church vision? Traditional churches that have embraced the cell structure are successfully transitioning to the cell model. However, in their initial attempts, some flourish while others often struggle to survive. What makes the difference? In researching their successes and mistakes, I offer this advice to churches in the challenge of transitioning . . .

### I. Check Your Motives

Why do you really want to become a cell church? Are you simply jumping on the cell bandwagon or desire a growing, effective church?

There is only one valid reason to pursue the cell model — obedience. You must have a burning vision from God for expanding evangelism and body life. You must be so completely convinced of the vision that when you utterly fail, you will get up and try again. If your motive is anything other than obedience, don't do it.

You will inevitably face obstacles and setbacks. If you are in this for self-advancement, you will eventually quit. This new model demands personal sacrifice and reorientation. The implementation of the cell model is a costly and involved process. Yoido Full Gospel Church in Seoul, Korea claims 800,000 members in cells, but learning and establishing the cell model was a big struggle for them from their initial implementation in 1964. It took ten years before a majority of their membership were in cells.

If you really want to become a cell church, first examine your heart and check your motives.

## II. Let God Change You

Are you reaching out, loving and sharing Christ with the lost? Are you praying regularly?

The cell model involves more than structural change. It requires a repentant heart. It needs concerted prayer and lifestyle evangelism. If you are a leader, don't expect your church to live these values unless you live them yourself.

How much time do you spend in prayer everyday? If you spend twenty minutes or less a day in prayer, you are living a "subnormal" Christian life. Start living a normal Christian life and take generous amounts of time with God. I do not suggest a legalistic monitoring of the time you spend in prayer. What I am challenging you to is a prayer-based life. This is a life where you love to spend time with God, interceding and hearing His voice.

"Ask and it will be given you; seek and you will find; knock and the door will be opened." (Luke 11:9) Remember this . . . *no prayer = no power; little prayer = little power; much prayer = much power.*

Forget transforming your church if you don't want to be transformed yourself. Get serious with God. Repent. Pray. Be Jesus to sinners. Let God change your life.

## III. Preach Values Before Vision

Many leaders make the error of "over-preaching" the cell vision. God places a new vision in their hearts for evangelism and the New Testament body life expressed in cells. As they catch this vision, they impulsively share their excitement by preaching and teaching about the impressiveness of the cell model, disregarding their early stages of the cell journey. However, there are no cells for people to join! In fact, it may be years until people can respond to their enthusiasm by joining a cell. This can be compared to software companies that announce fantastic new products that aren't anywhere close to being released. The result is frustration.

Don't preach about anything people can't grasp. Teach the values first, not the vision. The values of a cell church boil down to three essentials: prayer (loving God), body life (loving each other), and evangelism (loving the lost). These are basic New Testament principles, so don't preach "cells"; preach the Bible!

Start equipping your leaders and your members in relational

evangelism prior to cell involvement. Preach on body life and the power of prayer. The foundation of a cell church is its values not its structure. Lay this foundation well.

## IV. Start Small

A Chinese proverb declares: "The journey of a thousand miles begins with one step." Jesus emphasized the power of small beginnings. *"The kingdom of heaven is like a mustard seed, which a man took and planted in his field. Though it is the smallest of all your seeds, yet when it grows it is the largest of garden plants and becomes a tree, so that the birds of the air come and perch in its branches."* (Matthew 13:31-32).

Start small before you launch the entire church into cells. Experience the cell life yourself by beginning a proto-type group with a core of leaders and their spouses. Too many churches try to transition into a cell model by hastily training leaders and starting as many groups as possible. This doesn't work! This will not speed the process but slow it down.

Car makers prototype a new model before they mass produce. This enables the makers to work out the bugs, to improve the different components and see how they fit together. If a car is not protoyped, expect numerous factory recalls. Churches that rush into the cell model by skipping this phase and going directly to mass production will experience numerous recalls as they discover training gaps and other missing components.

You have a lot to learn. A cell group is more than a meeting. It involves community building, equipping, relational evangelism and raising leaders. Expect and pray for the difficulties in the initial groups. This is the purpose of prototyping — to discover and learn how to resolve problems.

## V. Multiply Leadership

As you learn how cells work, incorporate your future leaders into the start-up groups to experience cell life for themselves. Throughout and beyond the transition process, you must constantly identify and equip leaders. The cell model is not a small group strategy; it is a leadership strategy. The focus is not to start home groups but to equip an expanding number of caring leaders. If you succeed at this, your church will flourish.

In the cell model, every leader at every level must constantly observe how to multiply itself. Think, pray, and plan "leadership."

## VI. Pray, Pray, Pray!

Many pastors and leaders justify being too busy to pray. Their ministry pattern runs completely counter to the model of Jesus Christ. He too was busy, but He set time aside to seek the face of God the Father. Many people and needs were clamoring for His attention, but *"Jesus often withdrew to lonely places and prayed."* (Luke 5:16)

This life of prayer demonstrated by Jesus was captured by the early church. As the early believers constantly joined together in prayer, the Holy Spirit came with power. In the book of Acts, we read that miracles happened when God's people prayed. Salvation, the empowering by the Spirit, release of prisoners, appearance of angels, direction, visions, signs and wonders were continually given in response to prayer.

I have often said that the cell system is like an extension cord. If you plug it into God's power on one end and the needs of the world on the other, you will see an amazing flow of power. Unplugged, it is worthless.

Don't get serious about cells unless you are willing to get serious about seeking God in prayer.

## VII. Desire to Learn

Successful cell pastors have an eager desire to learn. They are constantly looking for new insights on how to improve ministry and cell life. They are humble and acknowledge that they have a lot to learn. They don't mind learning from people in other denominations, other countries or from younger leaders.

Successful leaders go to great lengths to learn. They travel to other churches, read books voraciously and attend conferences. They personify the exhortation in Proverbs 2:4 to seek for wisdom "as for silver and search for it as for hidden treasure."

Wisdom is imperative to radically alter the way you and your church do ministry. How impassioned is your search for wisdom? How eager are you to learn? Embrace an *insatiable* desire to learn.

## VIII. Increase Training

If you are moving to the cell model you must allocate more human and financial resources to equip leaders. Equipping leaders consumes more attention in a cell-based church that in traditional churches. As you mobilize more leaders, training intensifies. A careful examination of Jesus' ministry in the Gospel of Mark conveys that He spent 49 percent of His time in leadership training — interacting, teaching and mentoring the inner circle of twelve disciples.

Leadership training in a cell church is more comprehensive than offering classes. It begins in the cell with one-on-one equipping of each member. As persons are involved in ministry, the cell leaders and their coaches are constantly looking for caring and responsible members with leadership potential. Invite potential leaders (and their spouses if married) to a Cell Leader-Intern weekend. In this retreat setting, the expectations for training and shepherding a cell are surveyed. Those that continue are equipped in an intern class, while they become more involved in the ministry by their own cell leader.

A combination of modeling and instruction prepares leaders for the expanding ministry at all levels of the cell church. Do not look for shortcuts in your training and support system. The strength of the church will depend on the number and strength of the leaders, which will rely on the strength of your training.

## IX. Eliminate the Competition

Churches flounder in implementing cells because they want cells along with everything else they have been doing. Larry Stockstill, pastor of Bethany World Prayer Center in Baker, Louisiana, (a successfully-transitioned church) says it well. "It is hard to be on a diet and eat your regular meals too." You can't do cells along with everything else a church normally does.

Yonggi Cho, pastor of Yoido, echoes the same truth. "You must change the basic structure of your church. Many churches are failing in their cell ministry because they have not changed the basic church structure, for instance: Sunday School, Women's Department, etc. You can't graft the cell system into the old, traditional church ministry. This structure must be changed. This change is very difficult. If you don't change the basic structure, then the cell system will only be an added ministry to your church which will soon fizzle away."

Why are these cell pastors so adamant about eliminating the competition to cells? If you have extensive programming besides cells, these programs will contend against the cell system for time, leadership and prayer. If you deplete your leadership pool with other programs, your cells will get too big and won't be able to multiply. They will stagnate.

Eliminating those existing programs must be done carefully and prayerfully. If it is not done, your cells will fail.

## X. Love People More Than the Vision

One of the biggest mistakes leaders of transitioning churches make is loving the vision more than the people. Sometimes the vision becomes so important to them that people are seen as a means to its end.

The Pharisees exalted God's law to a lofty position. They thought people existed merely to serve the law. Jesus had the reverse mind set. He declared, *"The Sabbath was made for man, not man for the Sabbath."* (Mark 2:28) The same can be said for vision. The vision is made for people, not people for the vision!

As you dream big dreams, let God expand your capacity to care. Follow these commandments, but don't forget the greatest commandment to love God with all your heart, mind, soul and strength and to love your neighbor (and members) as yourself. If you really want a cell church, you'll love and hate the process. It is stretching, frustrating, disappointing — but exciting! The bottom line of the cell model is releasing people to minister, to edify one another and to reach the lost. If God tells you to do it, do it! Obedience is the key to Godly success.

# 6

## If I Could Do It All Over Again
### The Confessions of a Cell Church Planter
by David Buehring

*Dave Buehring currently serves as a Pastor at Belmont Church in Nashville, Tennessee, where he oversees the areas of Equipping and Leadership Development. He is also an author, a co-founder of Messenger Fellowship, as well as the Artist Pastor for World Vision's Artist Associates Program. He lives in Franklin, Tennessee, with his wife, Cheryl, and their two teenage children, Ryan and Malia.*

As a fifteen year veteran of missions, church-planting and pastoring, I have observed a tremendous need for a fresh understanding of community. This is the missing ingredient needed to experience what God has commanded us to do. I am convinced the cell model is the way to experience true community from personal experience and what I glean from God's Word.

I have seen the incredible impact that cell life has upon a town, city, nation or even an unreached people group if it includes deliberate discipleship and evangelism. As I read my Bible I see that this was the pattern used by Jesus and New Testament believers as they lived in a true attitude of community, prayer, discipleship and evangelism. From a church planting perspective, I thought this was wonderful. God placed within me the vision for a "multipliable-model" of church life that was based on a scriptural pattern and could be used to impact the nations of the earth!

With all of this stirring inside of me a few years ago, my wife and I launched a weekly meeting with a small group of friends for worship, prayer and applying the Scriptures to our lives. Through this weekly interaction, we learned how to truly love and care for one another. As we began the process, others were added to the group including a retired pastor and his wife.

He merged his little congregation with our budding cell church (now called a trans-plant: a pure cell church mixed with a group of people whose values needed to be transitioned). During that first year, God graciously blended us together into one precious community of believers, bringing Jesus all the glory. Without a doubt, our sense of community was our greatest strength. It was also the essential ingredient on which to establish a cell church.

As I look back over these past four years of pioneering (or trans-planting) a cell church, I know much of what we have done has been very effective and multipliable. However, there are also many things that I would do differently if I were to start over. Through my own failings and experiences as well as the input of many patient friends, I have learned much. In light of this, I'd like to share with you the ways I would go about pioneering a cell church differently if I could do it all over again.

### Pray, Model Prayer for Others, and Then Pray Some More!

All successful cell churches run on God's power, flowing through time spent in prayer. Cells may be the wheels that the church runs on, but prayer is the fuel in the tank! Early in my work, I developed a "pattern for prayer" for individuals and families based on the Lord's Prayer (Matt. 6:9-13). I chose those who felt a call from God as intercessors. I met with this group monthly to pray for our leadership and Body. Looking back, I would add these four elements that were missing from my original pattern:

- *Pastor's Prayer Life* - I would allow God to grow me beyond where I was at the time so that I might have better modeled it to those around me.
- *Leadership and Staff Prayer* - I would spend more time in prayer with my leadership team and staff, including an occasional prayer getaway.
- *Corporate Intercession* - I would begin by teaching on and taking the time for team intercession during our Sunday Celebrations as well as setting aside periodic half-nights of prayer.
- *Prayer Walking* - I would encourage my cells — right from the start — to commit to regular prayer walks in their neigh-borhoods. Asking God for His blessings and strategy for winning the lost souls living around them would have been powerful.

Even though we devoted long blocks of time fasting and praying over our trans-plant, looking back I would have spent even more time laying down this kind of foundation. Instilling the true value of prayer into the lives of those in our first cell would have given us a greater sense of God's heart. If I do it again, I will look for ways to help people catch a "spirit of prayer" that will become a *permanent* part their daily lives as the first step in cell church planting.

## Scriptural Ownership

Launching out on our journey into "cellular thinking," the Scripture became our guidebook. We taught those in our first cell what the Word said about living in true Christian community. We took our model from Acts 2:42-47, where we found many of the vital ingredients of what we wanted in our "multipliable" model. It is one thing to teach these things and quite another to see the vision of the cell church translated into the lives of the people you are leading and serving. That's the difference between just borrowing someone else's vision versus adopting the vision as your own. If the core member can't see it by revelation, imparted by God from His Word, he or she will not rise and take ownership as the pastor attempts to implement the process of planting a church.

I wanted to help people come to a point where they were convinced that the vision was from God and not just from me. After all, what use is a vision if it doesn't outlast the visionary? If they don't see it as a God-given calling they will not own this pattern of church life very long.

If I were to do it all over again, I would encourage those in our prototype cell to personally invest more time studying the Scripture portions outside of our weekly meeting. Then the same vision God had given me of the church would become a passion for them as well.

## More Modeling

In the Christian culture of our day, much of our training as believers involves sitting in class rooms with our Bibles, textbooks, notebooks and pens. While the blessing of this type of learning has filled our heads with wonderful information, it has horribly failed us when it comes to seeing lives transformed!

When Jesus called His disciples, He called them to "be with Him" (Mark 3:14). They walked, talked, ate, played and prayed as a group. They did everything together! Except for his own private times with the Father, Jesus always had two or more disciples with Him. This was not just a classroom experience; this was life experienced with Jesus. As we look at the gospels, we see that Jesus imparted His vision and Kingdom values to His disciples through *modeling*.

It has been stated repeatedly that much of what we learn is "caught" rather than taught. This essential part of disciple making is time consuming and uses a greater amount of one's energy than gathering a group into a classroom once a week.

The end result is the development of deep, godly relationships and the modeling of Jesus' character, attitudes, and ways. Jesus taught His disciples to invest in others. Paul learned and transferred this as seen in II Timothy 2:2 (Paul to Timothy; to faithful men; to others). Therefore, it is the way today's leaders need to do it too!

Substantial time investment in people can get rather messy and is often inconvenient for the average pastor. It also makes the pastor take a good look at his own life. He can only invest into others what he lives himself and give away what he is currently doing. If we want to produce Jesus-style disciples, then we must get back to life transformation as opposed to simply dispensing information.

As a communicator, I enjoy equipping people in my role as a preacher/teacher. But if I were to do it all over again, I would invest half of my time and energy into the lives of 6 to 12 of my key leaders. I would increase the time I spent with them praying, ministering, playing ball, etc. I resolve to "hang out" with my key leaders next time around and give them ample opportunity to be with me in a variety of settings. As a pastor, I now schedule less time in my office and more time with our present and future leaders. I wish I had started the church this same way.

### The Skillful Implementation of Vision and Values

Have you ever noticed that what you value is what you pour your time, energy and resources into? Consider your time: how much of it do you spend on the job or making money? How much time is given in prayer and meditating upon God's Word? How about time with your spouse and kids? What percentage of your life is deliberately involved in extending God's Kingdom?

We all live out our daily lives from within a basic set of values. As a leader, part of my role is to help people move from a worldly value system to a place of walking in step with Jesus. Helping our members to "seek first the Kingdom" and assist them in seeing how this plays out in cell life is a huge undertaking.

As change occurs, people will fall into one of the five categories below. Observe the chart and consider where your own key leaders might be. Then, choose the steps needed to help them align to the changes God wants to implement, related to their values and/or to internalize the cell church vision. As the chart shows, your leadership must be graciously moved from left to right. Please note that it is not unusual for this process to take from 1-3 years, depending on each individual and the size of your church.

While this may frustrate or discourage you, continue to pray and lead them to a place where they are able to integrate the value changes and your God-given vision for the church. Statistics imply that you can expect about 16% to flow with you quickly, followed by another 34% about 6-12 months later. Another 34% may take up to three more years to make the necessary adjustments. Also, don't be surprised if you lose some people who just choose not to align themselves to the Kingdom values found in cell life. Continue to love and bless them, knowing that God will pursue them in His own way.

My first years as a church planter have taught me that modeling Kingdom values for our people is my first priority. Once a person's values are aligned with the kingdom, they will freely gave their time, energy and resources. This shift will bring passion for prayer and equipping, for walking in community with others, and for reaching out to unbelievers.

Values implementation has always been paramount with our church plant. However, if I could do it over, I would have led our folks through a more deliberate process of seeing their values change while simultaneously catching a vision for the cell church.

## Picturing A Prototype

Like most cell church plants, we started out with a single cell. It was a healthy cell with precious people practicing real community. We remained together for eight months and then multiplied into three groups. One of those groups lasted three months and died. The other two continued to grow and multiply because they practiced community. We were off to a good start!

Eighteen months and several multiplications later, I realized that the saying, "you multiply what you model" was really true. Even though we were enjoying the blessing of God in our relationships with one another in cell life, I was concerned.

Some of our cell leaders ran with the idea of implementing an equipping track and others didn't. Meanwhile, the emphasis on evangelism and prayer for the lost was less than I desired. In addition to this, I discovered the discipling of future leaders by our current cell leaders was very weak.

This was a reflection of my own modeling, or lack of it, in this case. It showed me the need to begin with a prototype cell that can be an example for everyone of what cell life is all about.

If I ever plant another church, I will develop an initial cell that will have all the necessary ingredients to be healthy and to one day multiply itself. I see these basic ingredients as:

- Experiencing community that loves, cares, serves, allows people to move in their gifts and holds one another accountable.
- Applying God's Word to our lives.
- Actively reaching out to prodigals and unbelievers.
- The discipling of each cell member as well as future cell leaders, zone leaders, etc.

Given the opportunity a second time, I would have asked for input and listened to those who walked with me in the prototype cell to a greater extent. Their input was valuable and I found that giving them the opportunity to share their thoughts gave a greater sense of ownership in the overall vision of the church.

Walking through the days in my mind, I would now take more time with my initial cell. I would choose five or six other couples and walk with them closely for a full year until the Lord clearly gave us a green light to add others. We also needed to take on evangelism efforts and bring lost people to Christ and disciple them from the first day.

During that first year, I would make sure that all the ingredients listed above were added as a regular part of our lives. In this way, we would have all carried the same picture of how a cell should look and feel. This would have insured that future cells would function just like the original prototype.

## Actively Engage In Evangelism
## Right Away

The main reason we have been left on this planet is to bring much glory to Jesus. I see this being expressed in two ways: allowing the Father to conform us more and more into the image of Jesus and to reach those who don't yet know Him. When we look like Jesus to the world around us, His love will draw people to Him through us!

The cell-celebration structure is beautifully designed to harvest prodigals and unbelievers, see them mended, equipped and mobilized to reach others. I taught and encouraged the people in our body how to pray regularly for and to reach out to their *oikos*, or sphere of influence. We also had an outreach for the neighborhood on the front lawn of the school where we hold our Sunday celebrations. We have participated in mobilizing our cells to serve as servants for three weeks when Kurdish refugees were arriving in our city from Iraq.

This has all been good, but as I look back on it now, evangelism was initiated about two years too late! Because it was not actively engaged in with a sense of intensity by the initial cell under my leadership, that very important part of cell life was not viewed as the norm by all of our future cell leaders.

If I had another shot at it, I wouldn't change what we have done, but I would have done it in my prototype cell. I would have planted a two-fold vision for reaching out to our oikos individually and a monthly cell outreach of some kind. We would have walked the neighborhoods of our members, praying for each family, and asking God for his strategy to reach them. We would have reached out as a cell to the unreached people group living in our city. And last, but not least, I would have poured into them through modeling and teaching that evangelism is not an option, but a normal and vital part of our cell life together.

I know now that if I had implemented evangelism in my prototype cell as described above, my core leaders would have seen an obvious need for our equipping track. Even the smallest amount of successful evangelism leaves a discipleship hole that must be filled.

## His Presence First; His Structure Second

In the New Testament, Jesus talked about wineskins. These goat-skinned containers were made to keep fermenting wine. A new wineskin would be elastic enough to stretch with the pressure of fermentation. An old, stiff wineskin would burst when the new wine was poured into it. As we all should know, the important element in all of this is not the wineskin — it is the wine. The wineskin provided a structure, but it was the wine itself that was the prize. Just as a wineskin exists to contain the wine, so the cell church structure exists to contain the corporate expression of the presence of Jesus!

In the midst of our pioneering, the experience God was giving me regarding the cell church model overpowered my understanding of the reason for the new structure. It is meant to contain within its members the very presence of the New Wine of which the world needs to drink. The structure by itself will not produce life. Only Jesus can do that! While I fully understand this now, if I were to do it all over I would allow the structure to simply facilitate and contain what God was doing in our midst. The key here is to pursue Jesus and His presence first.

## Experimental Freedoms Within the New Wineskin

While establishing this multipliable model, I found it necessary to define the "core ingredients" needed to establish a well-founded and fruitful cell church. Some parts were essential to the success of the model and others could be modified or delayed without risking failure. As a result of this process, I have developed what I refer to as a "cell system" which serves as a foundational footing from which we operate. Of course, this takes a variety of people with unique gifts and callings who find their place in this model. People are the key ingredient!

To replicate this model in the nations of the earth, a common understanding of the essential parts must be understood by these unique individuals. From my perspective, the essential core ingredients of a cell church are:
1) Walking in the values of the Kingdom from the Scriptures.
2) Empowering it through worship and prayer, seeking and obeying God.

3) Experiencing relationships and community via living a cell lifestyle.
4) Every believer is mended and equipped to use their gifts in disciple making.
5) Leaders and ministries are constantly and deliberately developed and released.
6) The Kingdom is advanced by cells and its members reaching unbelievers in their *oikos*.
7) The leaders need to prayerfully strategize and organize to mobilize.

When we first multiplied our prototype cell, I was determined to differentiate the non-negotiables of a cell meeting and what could be "played with" by a cell leader. As I looked down the road, it was clear that we had to have a model that was easy to replicate. What I envisioned was to have the look and feel of cell #1 show up in cell #12 and so on. I knew this would provide for the effective training of sponsors, cell interns, zone leaders and even missionaries.

To help us do this, we implemented within each typical cell gathering what we refer to as the "4 W's" (*Welcome, Worship, Word,* and *Witness*). Each time we meet for a weekly meeting, the appropriate amount of time is given to each. This has been very helpful and although we were in different cells, we all walked through cell life at the same pace.

While I wouldn't change the 4 W's, I would have provided our cell leaders with more freedom within these guidelines as the Holy Spirit leads. For example, one cell may choose to function as an intergenerational cell while another may focus on certain age groups or specialized people groupings, etc. I would encourage our leaders to allow other cell members—not just those they had chosen to train as future leaders — to take turns facilitating the 4W's based on their giftedness and callings. Pastoral types should be encouraged to lead the *Welcome* and *Word* portions while evangelism-oriented people would lead the *Witness*, etc.

It has taken a few years to learn, but I have come to realize that if I establish a deep relationship with trained leaders they can be trusted to experiment within the boundaries of our vision. Because of the decentralized leadership base of the cell church, there is a potential for someone to stray with a part of the flock. This is where time invested in relationships, proper discipleship and leadership training will pay off. The constant visioncasting I do with our entire leadership and body in our celebration service also reduces the risk of a renegade leader. Because God wants maximum ownership of His vision, I know I have to make room for leaders with godly ideas of their own.

## Simplify the Vision So That Anyone Can Run With It

As I studied the model and sought God relating to the functions of the cell church, I felt I needed to write down what I was learning. In the process of doing so, I found that a whole notebook of valuable and pertinent foundations, principles and practical information was emerging that could help others.

To aid those who were working alongside me in this pioneering effort, I created a leadership notebook and asked every one to study it, along with Ralph Neighbour's book, *Where Do We Go From Here?* I was excited and wanted to pass on all that I was learning and had compiled! After a short time, I discovered that only a few had read the material while the majority of them were overwhelmed with the sheer amount of new information.

If I could do it all over again, I would find simple ways to communicate the principles and truths related to cell life. One of the geniuses of the cell structure is that the membership is able to carry much of the responsibility and authority within the local church setting. This allows them to grow and mature via hands-on ministry and leadership experience. With so much going on at home, with friends and on the job, there is a need to break these concepts down into bite-sized pieces so that they can taste it, digest it and use it as energy.

Books and binders full of information related to cell church life are still very important for study and as a resource. But if you really want to make your cell church hum, find ways within the unique culture of your local church to help leaders embrace and communicate the vision, principles and practical aspects. If I knew then what I know now, I would have very carefully considered this in prayer and sought advice from the people God had initially brought to walk with me in our pioneering effort.

## Take More Time To Learn From
## Those Ahead of You

As a leader, it's easy for me to run with something once I see what God is doing. Rather than just taking someone else's ideas wholesale, I like to develop some of my own. This is especially true in the area of developing training events and materials to disciple and equip leaders. I believe that when any of us takes ownership of a vision that God has imparted deeply inside us, we like to see how our own experiences, gifts and call will shape it. This ultimately puts your own unique "godly thumb print" on it.

I think God encourages us to do this at the proper time, but disregarding the materials of someone who is several steps ahead of you in the process is a waste of valuable energy that could be poured into people instead of printed paper.

When we began, the only helpful resource we could find was Dr. Neighbour's books. Beyond that we had to operate out of prayer and the fear of God. We took steps in what we thought was obedience learning from our mistakes while we journeyed into the cell model.

Fortunately, the Belmont Church of Nashville had begun the transition from a program-based design to a cell model just six months before. Thankfully, the pastor allowed me to be included in their pilgrimage and he let me contribute those things we were learning as well.

Today, there are many resources available for those led by Jesus to either plant or transition to the cell model. Hundreds of transitioning church pastors are delighted to take you under their wing! I was three years into our work before I attended *Advanced Cell Training* from TOUCH which literally showed us how to get from A to Z as it relates to the cell model.

If I could give you a recommendation, I would suggest that you introduce yourself thoroughly to the model and consider aligning yourself with a pastor and church who have already been doing it for a couple of years before launching out on your own. Later on, you will consider yourself wise if you can look for someone who is ahead of you in pastoring a cell church. Choose to walk in humility, and ask for a portion of their time, help and counsel.

I am very thankful to the Lord for the opportunities He has provided for me to learn about Him and His ways during the pioneering of the church where I serve. The tremendous team players God has brought to walk alongside us have been patient and trusting. We have indeed grown together in the exciting vision of the cell church. If I ever have the privilege of starting a cell church again from scratch, I know I will re-read this article as a refresher to get us off to a good start!

# 7

## 6 Powerful Reasons to Base
## Your Cells on Prayer
by Larry Stockstill

*Larry Stockstill has been on staff at Bethany World Prayer Center in Baker, Louisiana, since 1977 and became senior pastor in 1983. His ministry emphasizes prayer, cell groups and missions. The church has nearly 6,000 members who meet in more than 600 "Touch Groups" throughout the Baton Rouge area. The church supports 75 missionaries and organizations in 23 countries. Larry and his wife, Melanie, have been married for 21 years and have six children.*

Twelve years ago we changed our name from Bethany Baptist Church to Bethany World Prayer Center because of our conviction that prayer had to be our focus. In 1983, we began a Saturday morning intercessory prayer meeting from 9-10 a.m. God spoke to us that our church was to be a center for intercessory prayer for the nations, and we established a twenty-four hour "World Prayer Center" to pray for our missionaries, pastors, and government leaders. This center has been in operation round-the-clock ever since, except for a brief period of remodeling.

In the summer of 1991 we established Gideon's Army, a 500-member prayer force. We sensed that the cell strategy was from the Lord, but that it must be birthed in prayer. In the very beginning, we established cells which met every other week for edification and every other week for evangelism (members would bring friends). But these cells were made up of people from Gideon's Army who were praying diligently through each step in the process.

It was after this foundation of prayer was established that we ventured forth aggressively into the cell structure in April of 1993. We have since seen the Lord establish over 250 cell groups among us in a one and a half year period. We believe this is because we showered every move in prayer, we knew God had spoken at each level, and we were determined that prayer would be the heart of it.

But there were practical, biblical reasons for this emphasis on prayer. Let's look together at six reasons to base your cell ministry on prayer.

1. *Prayer births things that God wants to do.* Prayer has the power to "birth" things. The church of the New Testament was birthed at upper room prayer meetings. I feel no church can transition into revival and the immense changes of cell structure without a prayer base.

I am not alone in this. Many great moves of God in history were birthed in prayer: the Moravian missions phenomenon, the Methodist church and its emphasis on praying, small groups, etc. Someone once said that we have gone from the *upper room agonizing* to the *supper room organizing.* Prayer is the *birthing* power of the church, for "as soon as Zion travailed, she brought forth her children" (Isa. 66:8). "Substance before structure" is a guiding maxim that reminds us that revivals are "prayed down and not worked up." All the cell structure does is divinely contain and protect the harvest — but cells will not provide the harvest. One trip to Korea and Prayer Mountain should be enough to convince any pastor that cells do not *bring* the revival, they *hold* the revival. To see thousands of Korean intercessors at Prayer Mountain in the middle of a weekday on their faces praying for souls or to pass by a little prayer grotto and see a pair of shoes outside while a powerful intercessor inside is crying out for revival will be enough to reveal to you in what direction we should move.

2. *Prayer helps isolate the committed core of your cell ministry.* Think about it: what activity in your church trims down the attendance more than a prayer meeting? I have learned that the strongest disciples are those who long for the presence of God. Though you must occasionally endure some who are unbalanced, it is reasonable to say that your prayer warriors are the *committed core* of the church. They are also the most sensitive to the changing direction of the Holy Spirit in a church and most aware of the spiritual warfare necessary to birth something that is a major threat to satan's kingdom. Therefore, they will be the least resistant to change and the most resistant to demonic efforts to thwart the fledgling effort. Teaching your prayer core the principles of intercession and spiritual warfare equips them to be the leaders and reapers of the cell dynamic.

3. *Cells have the ability to do strategic spiritual warfare in prayer.* Located geographically, they provide the natural "command post" to do

spiritual "reconnaissance" for their particular area and engage those spiritual forces in intensive prayer battle. Much material has been written recently on how to do spiritual warfare for city blocks, neighborhoods, city zones, etc. Cell groups can do "prayer walks" and other intercessory activities to begin the process of loosening the strongholds of darkness over their area.

Because who better knows the particular spiritual strongholds of a neighborhood than those who live there? However, when most churches pray, it is for "the city" and is not informed, intelligent prayer for specific areas, like a street. We envision a time in the next three or four years when 1,000 prayer cells from Bethany and a host of other area churches work together to know each block of our city spiritually. There will be a group committed to interceding for that place daily. This strategy has been very effective in Argentina and other countries that are experiencing great revival through "prayer cells."

4. *Praying cells mean that the church-wide prayer load is evenly distributed.* We have discovered that a cell structure works because it brings "shared responsibility" instead of "volunteerism." In the prayer area, we share the load by assigning a section of three to five cells to be in our prayer room during each service, praying for the presence of God and for unbelievers to be saved. Led by the "Section Leader," the cells draw closer together as they intercede together. Then they actually provide the "altar workers" needed to reap the harvest at the altar call!

Also, the cells are each assigned to provide a "prayer covering" for one missionary family and one staff pastor (their District or Zone Pastor) through daily intercession. In this way, we know that all our missionaries and pastors have several groups calling out their needs continually before the Lord and are not lost in the shuffle without adequate prayer covering.

5. *Cells can focus on specific prayer objectives.* As the Senior Pastor, I have the vision of the current state of the church and the challenges we are facing in a particular month. The leaders hear the specific goals and urgent prayer needs that will affect the entire congregation from my vantage point and then communicate those prayer objectives to their cell groups. This means that the Pastor has hundreds of focused prayer warriors who are praying for the very

burdens he is continually lifting up before the Lord. Breakthroughs come quickly, and progress is never impeded.

6. *Cells can intercede for the harvest.* Our cell meetings operate on an alternating format: one week is edification, where believers minister in prayer to one another. The next week is evangelism, where unbelievers are invited and the lesson format is geared to specifically reaching them. During the "edification" week, the believers not only pray for each other's needs, but they break into "prayer triplets" and focus on three unbelievers each. The prayer triplet covenants together to pray for those nine names and then invites each to the "evangelism" meeting the following week. This prayer of agreement for the lost speeds up the harvest process, and now an average of 22-25 people are being saved weekly in the cell groups!

God brought an unexpected revival among us last spring as the cells prayed weekly for unbelievers. A drama came for a three-day performance in February and one thousand people came for salvation on the first night! The meeting went on for twenty-one nights, and a total of 18,290 people came forward for salvation and filled out decision cards. This was twice the harvest of the Baton Rouge Billy Graham Crusade! Our cell groups went quickly into action, each day following up the massive harvest and directing them to other area churches from which they had come or placing them in cells if they had no church. Some pastors, who did not even attend the dramas, baptized 25-30 new converts into their churches! This abundant harvest showed us the power of intercession for unbelievers and the crying need now in America to "get the nets ready." Harvest is coming to this generation as we have never seen or known, and we pastors had best be spending our time preparing our leadership to hold and conserve this coming massive harvest.

I challenge every church and every pastor to seek the Lord for a fresh outpouring in America before it is eternally too late. The dynamic of prayer when God moves in power is truly the only hope for this world. Prepare your church to be an engine of prayer that will open heaven over your city!

# Making Prayer A Priority

# Section 3

# 8

## Praying Heaven Open
by David Yonggi Cho

*Dr. David Yonggi Cho is the Senior Pastor of Yoido Full Gospel Church in Seoul, Korea. His congregation numbers over 800,000 members involved in more than 25,000 cell groups.*

It is refreshing to walk into a church and immediately sense the presence of God! It is also encouraging to be aware of the power of God in our daily lives over every situation. Both the refreshing and awareness of the power of God every day comes into our lives through prayer!

How can we develop a great desire to pray, that we may experience this power and reality in our churches and personal lives? I believe developing a great desire to pray is partially the result of knowing the purpose and benefits of prayer. That's the way God made us — we are motivated to do something when we understand its purpose and benefits. If we realize the benefits of prayer we will be a people of prayer.

To pray this way, however, means a change in our lifestyles. This change does not come easily and is uncomfortable. There are many examples, both Biblical and contemporary, of God's people acutely aware of the purpose and benefits of prayer.

Take the revival in Korea, for example. God has opened up heaven over Korea. I personally believe God is pouring out revival because our people have established strong prayer habits. Though they are already very industrious people, they have made prayer their first priority. By prayer they have communion and fellowship with the Holy Spirit. Today the Holy Spirit guides them in their daily living and they have power with God.

At Yoido Full Gospel Church, our people learned to pray in this manner. At first it was not easy, but as I led the way, they followed. We began with early morning prayer at 4:30 am. We added an all-night prayer meeting Friday nights from 10:00 pm to 4:40 am. Our people came to one or both prayer meetings. Although each person was on a different level of maturation, coming together strengthened us.

The fervency and persistence of the Koreans was an indication of the new place in prayer we had found. And this fervency was not unrewarded. One by one we prayed through to an overflowing experience of joy and faith and filling of the Spirit. We prayed through every visible and invisible hindrance before us. Lives were changed. There was an unseen high tide of faith and victory! The believers never went back to their passive praying, which is to pray only when one has time or feels like praying.

Neighbors and business associates saw the difference! The joy and peace and faith became contagious. Unbelievers were attracted to our church and when they came they accepted Jesus Christ as Lord and Savior. Prayer was the key that opened revelation of God's Word in their hearts as the Holy Spirit made the truth very clear to them.

This is why our church has grown monthly by an average of 10,000 to 11,000 members. We are now ready to pray with others for the many hundreds of prayer requests that come to us from all over the world. Prayer changed us and prayer has now changed the course of our nation.

In the Bible, examples of praying people are everywhere. These people knew how to pray. They prayed God down on their world, and He opened heaven to them.

For example, Moses had power in prayer. He could speak with authority not only to the enemies of God, but also to God's people. When he prayed, plagues came to Egypt. When he prayed, the Red Sea opened before Israel. When he prayed, God moved.

Joshua also saw the mighty hand of God work through his life and ministry. He knew the will and strategy of God in battle. Mighty cities fell before his untrained army. Where did this power come from? His prayer life! Joshua had learned to pray. While Moses was praying on the mountain, Joshua spent the night at the foot of the mountain in prayer. When Moses departed, Joshua was trained in prayer.

David was a man utterly given to prayer. When he was anointed king of Israel, Saul was still on the throne. David could have been discouraged by the fact that only a few recognized his kingdom, yet in prayer he came to a place of trust. He waited for the Lord to place him on Israel's physical throne. David was strong enough in his relationship with the Lord that he did not kill Saul when he had the opportunity. After Saul's death, David's first action as the recognized king of Israel was to bring back the Ark of the Covenant to its rightful place at the center of Israel's worship. When we look at the power in David's life and his kingdom, we see the source of his power: a life of prayer.

But no one has ever manifested the power of God like the Son of God, Jesus Christ. Before He entered His public ministry, He spent much time with the Father in prayer. This was the source of His power. He could do nothing unless the Father revealed it to Him.

Here in Korea, I have learned much from these examples of prayer in the Bible. I have learned that in my own personal ministry I must depend on the power of the Holy Spirit. It is not by might or natural power but by the Holy Spirit that great things are accomplished for God. I can pastor a church of over 800,000 and still have time to travel all over the world because I have power from the Holy Spirit in prayer.

As we pray there is a purpose: that God may be known and worshiped in the world. But when we pray the Holy Spirit also works on the one praying. One of the ways He works is by breaking us. Over the past 36 years I have learned that God cannot use a person who is not broken and completely surrendered to Him.

Look at the example of Peter. When Jesus met Peter in his fishing boat, Peter had one reaction: conviction. He felt as if he were too sinful for Jesus to be in his boat. Having denied Christ three times, he was broken by the grace and forgiveness of Christ. Peter was then used by Christ to open the spiritual door to the Gentile world. God was able to use Peter once he was broken. When a man is broken, his heart resists pride, and can be used greatly.

The Holy Spirit is the comforter. Yet, the comforter can make you most uncomfortable if you are not willing to be broken. The Holy Spirit ensures our obedience to the Heavenly Father by breaking us.

Another purpose of prayer is authority over satan. In this evil age, satan, supported by the fallen angels and demons is out to rob and destroy. Without depending on the power of prayer we are not able to break satan's power. The devil has never been concerned about church ritual, but he is deathly afraid of genuine prayer.

When you begin your life of prayer, you are going to discover new and diverse opposition from Satan.

How is this authority exercised in prayer? Satan opposes the prayers of God's people more than anything else. "For we wrestle not against flesh and blood but against spiritual wickedness in high places." (Ephesians 6:12) When Christ was crucified and resurrected He took the keys of death and the grave and declared "All power is given unto me in Heaven and in earth." (Mt.28:18). Jesus now shares His authority with you and me here on earth (Luke 10:19). As we learn how to pray in the Spirit, we realize we have been given Christ's authority, and with His authority operating in and through us we are able to bind the forces of Satan in people, cities, and nations.

How can we develop a great desire to pray? Know the purposes of prayer: that we might be changed, that the world might be changed. Then know the benefits of prayer: that God is victorious in all situations through our intimacy with Jesus in prayer, and He motivates us with dreams of what could happen through biblical and contemporary examples. When we experience the biblical dynamic of prayer in our lives we will then experience the refreshing and power of God in ways we never imagined.

# 9

## The Cell Church is a Praying Church
by Ralph W. Neighbour, Jr.

*Dr. Ralph W. Neighbour, Jr. has been a pioneering pastor, writer, researcher and teacher for over 50 years. He has personally tested his methods in many churches, including those in Houston and Singapore. He has written over 30 books that are used worldwide. He has held numerous teaching positions in seminaries and has consulted with churches on every continent. Currently, Dr. Neighbour continues to consult with churches and to develop useful materials to equip every member for ministry.*

I was 32 years old when I experienced the Lord in a life-changing time of prayer. It was triggered by a time of great anguish. I was scheduled to go to Suffolk, Virginia, to preach for an evangelistic campaign. During a time when racial prejudices ran deep, this was to be the first city-wide meeting co-sponsored by white and black churches. Then, at the last minute, the leadership of the largest white church in town refused to allow their church or their pastor to participate. As a result, that pastor asked me to come and hold a meeting for his congregation alone.

The spirit of hate was strong in the Sunday services! The people resented my presence, which convicted them of their decision to kill the crusade. After the Sunday services, I asked the pastor to leave me undisturbed in my hotel room until I called for him. I explained I did not know how long it would take, but I could not return to that pulpit until God showed me what to do.

I threw the key under the bed of my room, stretched out on the floor, and began to pray. Sunday night, all day Monday, and into Tuesday, I continued to fast and pray, agonizing over the situation of that church. I confessed my powerlessness to bring about change in those church members, and cried out for God's presence.

In the early hours of that second night, God came upon me. So heavy was His presence that I felt I could not catch my next breath! Waves and waves of His Spirit flowed into that room. When it was over, I felt totally exhausted, but I knew I had received His powerful presence and my preaching would never be the same.

Since the Monday night meeting had been cancelled, people

came in great numbers on Tuesday night out of curiosity. I don't think they knew that God was going to come in the power He did, but that packed auditorium met God in an encounter unforgettable. Repentance and confession of many forms of sin poured forth, and at 1 a.m. we were still meeting. I recall I was on my knees at the front row of pews with the pastor, and he whispered to me, "Ralph, I have never experienced anything like this! I am frightened. What should I do?" "Do nothing!" I whispered back, "God is bringing repentance, and we're not needed."

Little did I know back in those traditional church days that what we were experiencing then is what should be the norm for the Church. The manifestation of God's power is the heart of the Church's life. This means prayer should be the central focus of each cell group.

An examination of key cell churches in the world will demonstrate their common emphasis on prayer as the key to ministry.

When I attended David Yonggi Cho's Cell Conference several years ago, he launched it from Prayer Mountain instead of the lovely facilities of the Central Church on Yoido Island. The pastor of the world's largest church began his opening address by saying, "I have asked you to meet me here because I believe prayer is the most vital part of cell church life. This is my way of making that fact real to you." With that, the delegates spent several hours praying with him.

In the hours that followed, I walked past the prayer grotto which is reserved for Pastor Cho. We were told how he goes there on a Friday evening, to pray all through the night and into the next day.

In another visit, I made an appointment to see him. As we chatted, his secretary entered the room to inform him it was time for his next appointment. I dismissed myself and sat in the waiting room outside his office to wait for a friend coming to meet me. Curious about who his next visitor would be, I observed his office door to see who would follow me. Fifteen minutes later, no one had entered that door. Tactfully, I said to his secretary, "Has Dr. Cho's next appointment been delayed?" She smiled and said, "Oh, no. They are together now. You see, each day he uses this time to talk to the Lord."

The secret of his church growth was revealed to me by this experience. Dr. Cho has learned to prioritize the "Listening Room" in his life and ministry, to regularly be seated in the heavenlies to hear the Father's voice.

Over two million visits per year are made to Prayer Mountain by the members of his church. I have listened there to the wails of a broken hearted mother, praying hour after hour for a wayward daughter. I have heard the screams of a demon possessed man as he was delivered in one of the prayer chapels. I have watched the long lines of Christians lined up to be assigned a space to pray, holding a jug of water and a bed roll. At one sitting, I observed nearly 10,000 of his people gathered to pray on the upper level of the building there shaped like Noah's ark.

In the Ivory Coast of Africa, another significant cell church has grown to over 40,000. Pastor Dion Robert's schedule would cripple many men. He retires about 11 p.m., to awaken at 1 or 2 a.m. While the world around him is sleeping, he takes time to commune with his Master. His ability to hear the voice of the Lord in those night hours has guided his church since 1975.

With only eight hours' notice, Pastor Dion can assemble over 10,000 of his members for an all night prayer meeting. In preparation for their annual Easter harvest, 500 of his members lived in a stadium to fast and pray for ten days prior to the launch.

These two examples of cell church pastors reveal that prayer is the secret of the spiritual power in their churches. The anointing and harvest are results of their prayer lives. Prayer has produced the vision and passion that is seen in their cell groups.

My own experience within the cell church movement has revealed several levels of prayer activity taking place. These include:

## 1. Personal "Listening Room" Experience

In *The Arrival Kit*, cell members are trained to daily enter the "Listening Room," their time of prayer. They are encouraged to keep a journal to record impressions and thoughts which flow from His throne during those times. It is in the Listening Room that cell members first learn to hear from God and receive His guidance. Not only is his or her inner life strengthened by these experiences, but edification of other cell members begins with hearing from God about ministry to them.

The Listening Room experience differs from the traditional "Quiet Time." The awareness of the community, the cell, must be present in these intercessory times. The cell member's time with God is not a private event. He or she carries the needs of those in the basic Christian community to the throne of God, returning with spiritual gifts which can be released to meet the needs of others.

I recall an attorney in Fort Worth, Texas, who said to me, "I begin to prepare to edify the other members of my cell on the way home from each meeting. Through the week, the needs present in their lives is a vital part of my Listening Room times. By the time of the next meeting, I often have a special word from the Lord to build up a brother or a sister."

Further, the cell member becomes an intercessor for the unsaved. The *Share The Vision* times which conclude each cell meeting provide information about unbelievers who are being cultivated by cell members. Knowing that satan has sent the spirits of deception to blind and deafen the ears of all unbelievers, prayer for their release from this bondage is crucial. Cell members return to their homes with the information required to pray against the strongholds in the lives of unbelievers. It is because of these times of daily intercession that powerful grace begins to operate in the life of unbelievers. The needs within unbelievers is a daily issue for the cell member's prayer times.

## 2. Vital Cell Group Prayer Life

In the cell group meeting, prayer becomes a vital part of the worship and praise times. There may often be special moments as the group acknowledges the presence of the Holy Spirit. It is also a lovely experience to observe prayer in the Edification Time, as a group surrounds one of its members in a cell meeting, praying for physical healing or ministering to a serious problem.

Realizing that "our struggle is not against flesh and blood, but against the rulers, against the authorities, against the powers of this dark world and against the spiritual forces of evil in the heavenly realms" (Eph. 6:12), cell members must include prayer warfare as a vital part of their ministries. The domains of satan are penetrated by the prayers of believers, creating an atmosphere where spiritual freedom can exist.

Prayer walking is taught to cell members, and becomes a consistent practice for the group. For example, at Faith Community Baptist Church a special seminar was held to train all the cells to enter a geographical territory in prayer before entering it with share groups or interest groups. In Singapore, Faith Community Baptist Church sponsors zone prayer walks for its cells. Sometimes a cell will walk through the passages of the Housing Development Board flats, praying before each door. Most are marked by pagan symbols, including incense cans, images of gods, or mirrors to frighten away demons when the door is opened. With awareness of specific strongholds in the people living in each flat, prayer warfare can then precede each visitation.

### 3. Zone or District Prayer Journey

Zones or districts in some cell churches gather together on a regular basis (perhaps every six weeks) for a half night of prayer. The sessions begin with worship, testimonies from cells or members about what God has done through prayers for healings, deliverances, etc. After exhortation from the Pastor in charge, the groups may be given maps to designate areas for prayer warfare. In cars or on foot, clusters of cells will spend the evening, often past the hour of midnight, praying over the territory of the zones.

Special attention is given to areas to be targeted for the establishing of new cells. This joint effort increases the vision of the cell members to the district or zone as they pray. Special needs of the area are observed. In one such Prayer Journey in Singapore, kerosene lamps were observed burning inside large buildings under construction. An investigation revealed that there were several dozen indentured laborers from Bangladesh living in the space they were building. Out of this, a ministry has been generated to make contact with these workers and establish cell groups among them.

### 4. Church-Wide Prayer Life

Gathering together all the cells from the church for prayer is also vital to their work for the Lord. For example, every Friday night the facilities of the Central Church on Yoido Island in Seoul are packed and jammed with members coming for the half night of prayer. Twenty-five thousand or more gather for a meeting that begins at 8 p.m. and continues nonstop until 2 a.m. Singing and Bible teaching times are interspersed with the prayer times. Simultaneously, all the people pray aloud with great fervor. These prayer sessions may continue for 30 or 40 minutes before the leader rings a bell to call the audience to attention.

Faith Community Baptist Church in Singapore devotes a full hour of prayer in their worship services about once every three months. Everyone prays aloud at the same time. The pattern used for this 60 minutes includes ten minutes each for worship, prayer for the nation, prayer for the church, prayer for one's family needs, prayer for the unsaved, and prayer for one's own needs. This continual repeating of hour-long prayer times by the entire church is a powerful way to train cell members to pray for one hour.

When special events are forthcoming, church wide prayer vigils are held. For example, in December of each year Faith Community Baptist Church conducts an evangelistic harvest event called "Come Celebrate Christmas." In 1993, there were 48,000 people who attended this event. In September, at a prayer vigil people began to pray for one hour for every seat in the Singapore Indoor Stadium. Reports were received weekly from the cells of the number of hours the individual members had invested in prayer for this event. Thus, when the activity was held, every person sat down in a seat that had been prayed over for one full hour. The atmosphere of the event, from the first minute the auditorium was occupied, was charged with the presence of the Holy Spirit.

It makes a difference when prayer is a focal point of a church! When Peter Wagner came to speak for the Touch Equipping Stations classes, he remarked after his first three-hour session, "Speaking in this auditorium is amazing! Seldom have I experienced such freedom in my teaching. The atmosphere here is charged with God's presence as a result of your prayer lives."

## 5. Church Staff Prayer Life

Sadly, I have participated in religious organizations all my life, beginning with my early post-college years with Billy Graham and including denominational jobs and serving as pastor or staff member of Program Base Design churches. Not once was I exposed to the life of prayer as thoroughly inserted into a church staff as I have experienced during the past four years at Faith Community Baptist Church!

Each staff member is given three days of prayer leave every three months. A small stipend is given toward the rental of a hotel room, and staff go in pairs for this time of quiet meditation and prayer. While most of the time is spent alone, there are seasons of prayer and sharing between the two during meals.

The first Tuesday of each month, the 173 employees of the church begin a prayer season which goes from 8 a.m. to 1 or 2 p.m. Part of this time is spent praying individually, another part as an office staff event, and finally all the staff gathers for praise and prayer warfare which occupies the last hours.

The rest of the Tuesdays include a prayer meeting for everyone from 11 a.m. to 1 or 1:30 p.m. We often wrestle with problems the church is facing, and always pray for our cell church planters who have gone out from us to labor in Vladivostok, Alma Ata, Hong Kong, Indonesia, the Philippines, and among the restricted nations.

Each day begins with an hour of prayer within each department. Thus, the staff is saturated with prayer events that are done on "company time." It is my feeling that the reason we have gone for seven years without a serious problem between staff members is because of the prayer bonding that takes place on a regular basis.

Like a machine needs oil, so does a ministry or church need prayer. We must pray for God to anoint what we do. We should pray for God to touch every area of our ministries with His anointing. Charles Spurgeon once said, "I don't know what anointing is, but I know when it is not there." Do people sense this "anointing" in our lives, in our ministries and churches? Let us ask God anew for His help in not only our personal prayer lives, but also the prayer lives of those we minister to in the cell church.

# 10

## Touching The Heart of the True Shepherd
### How To Make Prayer the Center of Your Cell Leadership
by Karen Hurston

*Karen Hurston speaks and consults with churches internationally on prayer, cell groups and visitation ministry. She is the author of the excellent book,* Growing the World's Largest Church, *which documents the key growth elements of the Yoido Full Gospel Church.*

George and Sally Forrester often invited Ben and Nancy to their Columbia, South Carolina cell group. Ben and Nancy always refused. Rather than letting this discourage them, George and Sally committed to pray even more fervently for their agnostic neighbors. The Forrester's did not know that Ben and Nancy's marriage was extremely unstable. After a sharp disagreement, they felt there was no hope. They decided to see a lawyer the next morning to begin divorce proceedings. At that moment, George knocked on their door, trying one more time to invite them to their cell meeting. Ben shrugged his shoulders, glanced at Nancy and said, "Why not? It sure can't hurt."

To their surprise, Ben and Nancy found they enjoyed the warmth of their new Christian friends. But more importantly, they made the most vital decision of their lives. They repented of their sins, let go of unforgiveness and received Jesus Christ as Lord and Savior. Today, Ben and Nancy not only have a strong marriage, but also lead a cell group.

Bruce Klepp, pastor of Upper Room Assembly in Miami, Florida, smiled as he gave a testimony from one of their cell groups: "With the recent hurricanes we experienced, it has been almost impossible to sell homes. We've had a couple from one of the cell groups that has been desperate to sell theirs. It had been on the market for months with no results. Then they began hosting a cell in their home, and their group began praying for them. Within a few weeks, their home sold."

Ruth attended a cell group in rural Pennsylvania. During one cell meeting, she shared an unusual prayer request. Her daughter's car had struck an expensive bull on a gene farm. The bull had lain injured and paralyzed for hours before someone could come and help. The attending veterinarian said that the bull would not be able to walk for at least a year, and then only with expensive and time-consuming physical therapy. The group prayed that God would work His will in this situation with the wounded bull. After three weeks, the bull started walking, much to the veterinarian's amazement.

As a child, stories like these became normal for me. From age seven until 16, I grew up in Dr. Cho's church in Seoul, Korea. Later, I served on staff from 1976 to 1981, watching that church grow from 40,000 to 200,000 members. During my time there, I repeatedly heard testimonies of answered prayers in cell groups. Since then, as a traveling consultant and speaker — whether in Switzerland, America, Germany, South Africa or the Philippines — I continue to hear cell groups joyously tell of answered prayers. Jobless members find employment, broken marriages and relationships are restored, clear direction and wisdom are given and the sick are healed.

Being an effective cell group — a group that truly ministers in the name of Jesus Christ — is directly related to seeing God work through prayer. He does what no cell leader can do. Leading a cell group then is first and foremost a call to prayer, a call to communion with the good shepherd of your cell.

## Jesus' Example in Prayer

Jesus spent his life making prayer warriors out of twelve men. Prior to the calling of the twelve, Jesus spent all night in prayer (Luke 6:12). This, however, was not the only time that Jesus went off for extended times of prayer. Mark 1:35 says, *"And in the morning, long before daylight, He got up and went out to a deserted place, and there He prayed."* After feeding the 5,000, just prior to his walking on water, Jesus was alone in prayer. Before He did any of the above, He spent 40 days with God in the wilderness.

Jesus spent time alone with God in prayer, modeled prayer to his interns (remember the garden of Gethsemane?) and taught his group how to pray (*"Lord, teach us to pray, as John also taught his disciples."* Luke 11:1). Prayerlessness angered Jesus. In the temple, Jesus overturned the tables of moneychangers and the benches of those selling doves as he declared, *"My house is a house of prayer"* (Luke 19:46). Perhaps we could paraphrase Jesus today and say, *"My Father's cell will be a gathering for prayer."*

## Strengthen Your Prayer Life

Eight years ago, I had lunch with a lady who had been a section leader (equivalent to a zone supervisor) in Dr. Cho's church for more than ten years. As we sat before a plate of fruit, I asked this woman of God, "From what you have observed over the years, what makes the difference between an effective cell leader and an ineffective cell leader?"

She reflected for a moment and then explained, "It's really quite simple. The effective cell leader reads and studies the Bible more, prays more, makes more prayer visits and reaches out more to the lost. More time in the Word and in prayer is essential."

In his challenging book, *Home Cell Group Explosion*, Joel Comiskey points out four factors that relate to the leader's prayer life:

- "Those (cell leaders) who spend 90 minutes or more in devotions per day multiply their groups twice as much as those who spend less than 30 minutes."
- "Those who pray daily for cell members are most likely to multiply groups."
- "Spending time with God preparing the heart for a cell meeting is more important than preparing the lesson. . ."
- "Regular visitation by the leader to the cell members helps consolidate the group." (I would qualify this as prayer visits.)

In October of 1987, I surveyed more than 400 of the cell leaders at Dr. Cho's church. The typical cell leader prayed for an hour a day. More than half of those leaders also attended one all-night prayer meeting a week. In addition, many also fasted not just for struggling members, but also for targeted unbelievers. Many went to the church's prayer retreat, Prayer Mountain, for extended times of prayer and fasting.

## Pray With and For Your Intern

If the pathway to a praying cell starts at the door of the leader's personal prayer life, the next step of the journey involves modeling and leading your intern to pray. Jesus was constantly modeling prayer for his disciples. Even in the garden, where drops of blood poured forth in sweat, he was modeling prayer to his inner circle.

Pablo Fuentes is one of the best cell leaders I have ever met. In the past 29 years, Pablo has personally led over 19 cell groups in the northern California area. During that time, Pablo has raised up 27 new leaders and multiplied 22 groups.

How has Pablo been so effective? First, he begins every meeting with a clear vision statement that concludes with the importance of multiplication. He also prays weekly with his intern, usually after the cell meeting at a location away from the host home.

During this hour-long meeting, Pablo and his intern assess the last meeting, discuss what can be done for those in need of additional ministry, and plan prayer visits and evangelistic strategies in the group. Most importantly, they pray together. Pablo prays for the intern's personal needs, and together they pray for group members and for upcoming meetings and activities.

"More important than any task," declares Pablo, "is that the leader minister and pray for the personal needs of the intern. Many times we have spent our entire hour in ministry. Once personal ministry takes place, doing the task of leadership is much easier."

## Make Prayer Visits to Cell Members

How do you help your cell members appreciate the importance of prayer? The journey to becoming a praying cell greatly increases when the cell leader and intern make prayer visits to members. According to my survey of cell leaders in Dr. Cho's church, the typical cell leader makes an average of three to five prayer visits a week. This praying not only benefits the members, but also models prayer to them.

Steve Allen pastors Christian Outreach Center in Columbia, South Carolina. Recently, group leaders and other leadership at COC made prayer visits to more than 140 homes. "Even in our private American society," Pastor Allen states, "prayer visits in homes brings about a strong sense of *koinonia*. Prayer visits have given us a reference point to minister to those families that we did not have before. We were able to address specific needs through conversation and in prayer."

What do you do on a prayer visit? First, schedule the visit, clearly explaining that you will not be able to stay long. 30-40 minutes is sufficient. Tell them you just want to pray with them and bless their home.

On the actual visit, I use the acrostic "P-A-M." Begin with a brief word of *prayer*; this sets a spiritual tone to the visit. Continue by *asking* them how they are doing. Then ask, "Do you or your family have a need or concern for which we could pray?" After identifying an area of need or concern, then *minister* the Word. Find one verse or passage that matches the need or concern that has been shared. Have the person read that verse or passage, then spend two to five minutes encouraging them from that Scripture. Then minister in prayer. While the first prayer was brief and general, this prayer is lengthy and specific to the need or concern.

Up to this point in the prayer visit, ministry is directed to that person or family. Now ask, "Is there a specific unbeliever you want to see come to a saving relationship with Jesus Christ?" After identifying someone, join in a prayer of agreement for his or her salvation. Pray that God would use the person/family as an instrument in the process of bringing the unbeliever to the Lord. Conclude the visit with a prayer of blessing. Bless that person, that family, their finances, and their relationships.

These visits serve several purposes. As a leader, it keeps you in touch with the intimate needs of your members. It also gives you opportunity to model to the members how they are to pray and minister. Often the intern will accompany you, the cell leader, on the visit; this is a wonderful opportunity to grow in unity as you work together in ministry.

### Don't Give Up! Persist!

Will you see all your prayers answered in your cell group? Probably not. Following these steps does not guarantee automatic answers. Perhaps this is the reason why Jesus told the parable of the unjust judge in Luke 18. Rather than giving up, the widow kept coming to the judge with her plea. Even though the unjust judge did not fear God or care about men, he saw that she received justice because the widow kept bothering him. Jesus then stated, *"And will not God bring about justice for His chosen ones, who cry out to Him day and night? Will He keep putting them off? I tell you, He will see that they get justice, and quickly"* (Luke 18:7-8a).

I remember meeting the cell leader of a group outside West Palm Beach, Florida. His group made a written record of each prayer request, complete with date given, name of person making the request and an empty column to record the date of the answer to that prayer. Once a prayer request was given, the group continued to persist in prayer for that request until they heard an answer. After a year, they discovered that 90 percent of their prayers had been answered.

## Fall in Love

Have you ever been in love? Just the sound of the beloved's voice brings joy to your heart. You want to be close to him, even in a crowded room. When the love is reciprocal, you want to tell that person how wonderful he is and how much you love him. At other times with your beloved, you share your concerns and struggles, asking his opinion and viewpoints. On other occasions, you share your concerns about others.

That is the best picture of the cell leader's prayer life: the leader's prayer life is to be in the context of his love relationship with God through Jesus Christ. Spend time loving and worshipping the Lord. Share with God your needs, concerns and struggles. Share with Jesus your concern for others. That is the essence of intercession.

Jesus' first call to His disciples and to each cell leader is the same: "Follow Me" (Matthew 4:19; 8:22; 9:9; Mark 2:14; Luke 5:27; John 1:43; 21:19). Being a cell leader is more than just running a meeting, caring for members, reaching out to unbelievers and raising up new leaders. Being a cell leader involves praying to the Lover of our souls and the true Leader, the Good Shepherd, of our cells, Jesus Christ. He will do the impossible, like call your neighbors to repentance, sell the unsellable home, or heal a prize bull. You and your cell group can believe God in prayer like this. Start by asking!

# 11

## Drive-By Warfare
### Ganging Up On Satan's Turf!
by Randall G. Neighbour

*Randall Neighbour is the president of TOUCH Outreach Ministries and the Senior Editor of CellGroup Journal (formerly CellChurch Magazine). He and his wife live in Houston, and co-lead a cell group at Garden Oaks Baptist. His passion is helping his cell members enjoy a strong purpose in life by reaching the lost for Jesus.*

My neighborhood is an eclectic weave of run down rental property, renovated bungalows and new victorian homes located near downtown Houston. Although we live in the shadows of skyscrapers, the tree-lined streets and old architecture are reminiscent of a small town.

Because this area doesn't have the pristine look of a suburb with its deed restrictions and zoning, we are always on the watch when an entrepreneur chooses our area for a business venture. The sale of liquor was banned years ago to preserve the quality of life in this tiny community, yet the outskirts of the neighborhood are lined with many liquor stores and bars.

On my way home from work one night, I spied a foundation for a new building outside our neighborhood boundaries. As I sat at the traffic light, I wondered if it would be a bank or a new restaurant. Week after week, I watched the progress of the construction. The construction phases were fascinating to me, and each week's progress made me eager with anticipation.

The building's design and stucco facade told me a great deal of money was being invested into the property. All it lacked was a sign inviting me to become a patron.

A few days passed, and the business opened with signage of gigantic proportions. The owner purchased a billboard which loomed above the building. My anticipation instantly turned to disappointment and alarm when I looked up to see it was a topless nightclub called *The Wolf!* On opening night, businessmen from downtown Houston covered the parking lot with expensive cars like red carpet rolled out for the grand opening.

I was relieved to discover that I wasn't the only alarmed homeowner, and my neighbors and I had something else in common. We all wanted a nice neighborhood free of adult-oriented businesses and indecent nightclubs. Talking over the fence with them, I blurted out, "God will close that business, because I'm praying over it every day when I come home from work. Just watch and see." You can imagine the look on their faces! Tongue-in-cheek, they said they hoped I was right and that my prayers were effective. (My neighbors aren't Christians yet and nothing of what you'd call "prayer warriors" by any stretch of the imagination.) They suggested a call to the city council, but I knew the nightclub was well within the law. If I was to see any action, I was going straight to the Man Himself!

Just as God brought down a palm reader and a cult shop a block away from my home, I knew He would bring down this stronghold of satan's work. When I prayed against the palm reader, God's power overcame the power of darkness in just 10 days. I expected the same results with this topless bar. As I drove by that business every day, I shouted, "satan, you have no place in my neighborhood! Take your demons and this business and leave! By the power given to me by God through the shed blood of Jesus Christ, you must leave this area and go where Jesus tells you to go — never to return!" I was so focused on my mission that I didn't care what people thought of me as they saw me screaming at a building from my car!

Months of drive-by warfare with no visible results were not easy. I found out that some demons are more stubborn than others, but I remembered an important Old Testament truth. Jericho was a sizeable city, and it took a while for the walls to crumble. Numerous times around the property and an incredible faith on the part of God's army was necessary.

To be truthful, I was scared of the warfare arena. A friend told me stories of sudden illnesses, injuries and incredible confusion caused by satanic backlash. I knew satan would attack me when he realized what I was doing. I knew I couldn't go into battle without reinforcements. So, I shared my warfare strategy with my cell, and they agreed to pray when they passed the building. They also prayed for protection for my household and my ministry. With the prayer support of my cell, I stood firm knowing that Christ was behind me like a big Brother on the playground after school, ready to overpower the bully if he made one move against me.

Persistence and faith paid off. I watched the business lose its liquor license and make a last ditch effort to remain open by shifting to totally nude dancing. They lowered the cover charge and posted it on a large sign. The welcome mat of new and expensive cars in the parking lot soon changed to a worn out rug of older, less conspicuous cars. God brought them down!

Today I sit at that same traffic light and praise God for the "for sale" sign and the overgrown weeds. I also praise Him that my "pre-Christian" neighbors witnessed spiritual warfare and the power of God over satan. I thank Jesus that for the first time in a long time, I was not ashamed to look foolish for Him.

The next time satan decides to establish his turf in your neighborhood (and even in your own backyard), remember that your big Brother and mighty God, Jesus Christ, is right behind you with all the authority in Heaven. Feel free to shout, "Satan, you better think twice before messin' with my neighborhood! Jesus and His angels will drive you out! This is His turf — not yours!" You may feel stupid at first, but you will see God's victory in the end!

*"Finally, be strong in the Lord and in His mighty power. Put on the full armor of God so that you can take your stand against the devil's schemes. For our struggle is not against flesh and blood, but against the rulers, against the authorities, against the powers of this dark world and against the spiritual forces of evil in the heavenly realms. Therefore put on the full armor of God, so that when the day of evil comes, you may be able to stand your ground, and after you have done everything, to stand."* (Ephesians 6:10-13)

# Making the System Work

# Section 4

# 12

## 10 Ways to Refresh Your Church Atmosphere
### Is Your Church "Air" Appealing or Repelling?
### One Whiff Will Tell
by Ben Wong

*Ben Wong is the senior pastor at Shepherd Community Church in Hong Kong. He oversees 40 groups and 1200 people who attend worship. He also developed the Hong Kong Cell Church Network, which consists of 168 churches from 20 different denominational traditions.*

Vibrant cell groups are life changing. Non-Christians meet Jesus and are saved. People find honest and healthy friendships, sometimes for the first time in their lives. Others discover the meanings of grace and forgiveness, and learn how to extend these to others.

Does this describe your experience in small groups? Or does your reaction fall somewhere between "ho-hum" and "I'm sure glad that's over!"?

Being part of a small group, either for one visit or for the long-term, does not guarantee a great experience. Even churchgoers can come across as calloused or unfriendly. Cells are a way to organize a church body, but simply placing people in small groups doesn't mean they'll mature spiritually or become others-focused. If your church is dead, and you put a bunch of spiritually dead people into small groups, you will be an organized dead church. If your church is alive in God and adopts His values, your groups will resemble breaths of fresh air.

What is the atmosphere like in your church? Take a "deep breath" in your Sunday service and in your cell group. Does the atmosphere attract others? Do outsiders look in and see something they want? We sampled the air at our church, Shepherd Community in Hong Kong, after the cells started floundering. God revealed some poor "atmospheric conditions," and showed us that people were breathing polluted air that was choking the cells. We filtered and cleansed the air by applying some new values to our lives, and quickly saw change and growth.

Is your church's atmosphere as inviting as the fresh scent of a spring shower or as repulsive as the stench of a stagnant swamp? By measuring your church with the following ten atmospheric conditions, you will know how to bring new life to your group and church.

## 1. Have a Positive Faith in God.

God continually challenges us to enter the realm of the unknown. While you alone may not be able to do some things, if your instructions are from the Lord, you can accomplish them with His help. As Christians with the power of Jesus Christ, we are not confined by man's potential. Paul said, *"I can do all things through Christ who strengthens me"* (Philippians 4:13 [NKJV]).

When a difficult situation arises, press into it. If you tackle only those things with which you are comfortable, you'll never mature spiritually. God grows us when we live outside our comfort zone. For example, if a person is asked to be a cell leader and accepts the position believing that he can lead by his own knowledge and power, then he ought to do something else or he will stop growing. If, on the other hand, he knows that he cannot lead except by the grace of God, he should take the chance. If you face something and think, "I can't do it," then you must depend on Jesus to accomplish it through you.

God will lead you into tunnels with no light. So many times we focus on the darkness — problems, criticisms, fears — and we fail to hear the voice of God. He said, *"I have told you these things, so that in me you may have peace. In this world you will have trouble. But take heart! I have overcome the world"* (John 16:33). You will never do anything for God if you do not believe these words. He moves in the things that you alone cannot do, but you can boldly say, "Yes, I can, because God is on my side."

## 2. Make Church Fun!

To make church or cell meetings boring is a sin. God is anything but boring. Church should be fun and exciting, reflecting God's nature. People want to bring friends and neighbors to a fun church, not to one where they will fall asleep during the service. If newcomers enjoy your church, they will come back and bring others with them. If cell members leave a cell meeting wearing a bigger frown than when they arrived, they will stop coming.

Learn to distinguish between being serious and being solemn. We can be serious about God and our ministry and be "wild and crazy guys," too. It's OK for Christians to have a sense of humor. Chinese churches, for example, are traditionally very solemn. This creates heaviness over people, and people return to church only out of guilt or hurt. A fun church atmosphere is to a nonbeliever what a free gourmet meal is to a starving man. Who can turn it down? Break out from your old church mold!

### 3. Bring Out the Best in People.

Robert Rosenthal, a Harvard psychologist, and Lenore Jacobsen, a school principal in San Francisco, tried something novel. As primary school began, new teachers casually received the names of five or six students in their classes who were designated as "spurters" based on a test the year before. Though these students actually were chosen at random, the teachers believed they had exceptional learning abilities. The teachers described these selected students as happier and more curious, affectionate and apt to succeed than their classmates. The only change for the school year was the attitudes of the teachers.

The result: These five or six pupils in each class scored far ahead of the other students, gaining 15 to 27 IQ points over the previous year's test results. The study proved that the way we perceive people is the way we treat them, and that the way we treat them is the way they become.

Remember this important principle: You put people in touch with their faults when you assume a negative attitude toward them and reflect back to them only your perception of their weaknesses. Conversely, by assuming a positive attitude and concentrating on their strengths, you put them in contact with their good attributes. Their behavior inevitably improves. Proverbs 23:7 says, "For as a man thinks within himself, so he is."

### 4. Accomplish the Great Commission.

Jesus said in John 4:35, "Do you not say, 'Four months more and then the harvest'? I tell you, open your eyes and look at the fields! They are ripe for harvest." The fields Jesus referred to are in the world. The harvest is in the world, not in the church. Ideally, Christians go to church to get healed and encouraged so they can serve the Lord in the world, fighting the war against Satan. The church equips ministers to fight that war, and the world is the battlefield and our place of service.

Jesus told us in the Great Commission to "go." He did not tell the world, "Come to church." People all around us — co-workers, neighbors, 7-Eleven clerks, cousins, golf partners — live in darkness. How will they know about the Light of the World if we do not show it to them and tell them about it? Their bondage keeps them from coming to the place of truth. Therefore the church, YOUR church, YOUR cell group, must go to them.

A "go" atmosphere creates expectation and excitement, and transforms a dull Christian life into an action thriller. You find yourself waiting to see what God will do next. Start praying for, relating to and inviting the pre-Christians in your life and watch this aspect of your church attitude change.

## 5. Be a People of Destiny.

People, including many Christians, are dying for something to live for. Yet a large percentage of churches tell people to attend the Sunday service and the weekly cell meeting — period. Is this all there is to "church"? No! Everyone has a call on his or her life. God has called everyone into ministry. No one is excluded.

No one is in your cell by accident. Yet we often think people will reach their God-ordained destiny by accident. We get frustrated waiting for people to grow up. Shepherd Community has learned to prepare people to find and then attain their destiny. We equip them to live victoriously in Jesus' freedom, and we teach them how to reach non-Christians. We disciple people within the context of relationships so they can discover their destiny, their "something to live for," in the Kingdom of God.

We challenge people with a big vision. When I was a 6-month-old Christian, I started a weekly group meeting with six other young people. Some well-meaning Christians told me that I was supposed to grow up spiritually before I could help others grow. But I was being discipled by a friend named Peter, who showed me what being a Christian was about. Then I gave it to others. I saw God's vision for ministry very early, and I took the challenge even though it was risky and some said I was wrong.

## 6. Learn to Work Together, as a Team.

I alone am not a good pastor. I need others, a community, around me. I must work smarter, not harder.

When I assembled my leadership team for Shepherd Community Church, I looked for people who were different from myself. We are different in temperament and strengths, and we even look different. One has long hair and another prefers short hair. Some are modern, while others are more conservative. We have the jokers and the extra-serious.

God works through variety. Some in your cell group will be strong at prayer. Others will lead out in evangelism, or will have a deep knowledge of the Word. Learn to work with the diversity of giftedness surrounding you. Delegate tasks, and use people in their strengths. Don't try to do everything by yourself.

Shepherd Community succeeds because of the team, not because of one person, and certainly not just because I am the senior pastor. For example, Tony Chan wrote me a letter stating that his purpose was to help me be the best senior pastor in Hong Kong. What support and selflessness! That's what makes a successful team. United we stand; divided we fall.

To work together in unity, the team needs to submit to the leader. The leader needs to shepherd with love, but the followers need to submit. Without this dynamic, teamwork doesn't exist.

## 7. Learn to Fail Well.

Fake people hide behind faces and masks. Real people outwardly reflect what is going on inside them. The key to relationships is to be real. The Bible tells us to "walk in the light," and this means to walk in openness, to let others see our failures and weaknesses.

Failure is a prerequisite to success. All successful people fail, even the great people in the Bible (remember the mistakes that Moses and David made?). Leaders who go to great lengths to hide failures are foolish and hypocritical. Strong people make as many mistakes, and just as ghastly, as the weak people. The difference is that strong people admit them, laugh at them, learn from them. That is how they become strong and gain the respect of their followers.

Some managers refuse to accommodate failure, and they fire employees who stumble. But the best managers expect their people to make mistakes. Instead of replacing staff members, they teach employees how to cope with failure and how to learn from their mistakes. Leaders who impart perseverance and tenacity, and help others learn from their errors, perform a vital service while creating a superior organization.

Abraham Lincoln was a great U.S. president, but look at this string of failures: failed in business in 1831; defeated for legislature in 1832; sweetheart died in 1835; suffered a nervous breakdown in 1836; defeated for Speaker in 1838; defeated for Elector in 1840; defeated for Congress in 1843 and 1848; defeated for Senate in 1850; defeated for Vice President in 1856; defeated for Senate in 1858. If Lincoln had given up anywhere along the way, he may never have been elected President in 1860.

Where did Lincoln gain the ability to remain undeterred? From the people who believed in him when he lost, encouraged him when he despaired, taught him that failure is not permanent and pushed him to continue. We must surround God's people with the same level of encouragement.

## 8. Constantly Change for the Better.

Our God is the God of change and the new. His "compassion is new every morning" (Lamentations 3:22-23). God promises that the old things will pass away. Isaiah 43:18-19 says, "Forget the former things; do not dwell on the past. See I am doing a new thing! Now it springs up; do you not perceive it? I am making a way in the desert and streams in the wasteland."

When Jesus comes into our lives, He transforms us. "Therefore, if anyone is in Christ, he is a new creation; the old has gone, the new has come!" (2 Corinthians 5:17). Many people in your church or cell group can testify to the former and the current change in their lives.

A man once said, "I was a revolutionary when I was young, and my prayer to God was this: 'Lord, give me the energy to change the world.' As I approached middle age and realized that my life was half gone without my changing a single soul, I changed my prayer to this: 'Lord, give me the grace to change all those who come into contact with me; just my family and friends, and I shall be satisfied.' Now that I am an old man and my days are numbered, I see how foolish I have been. My prayer now is: 'Lord, give me the grace to change myself.' If I had prayed for this right from the start, I would not have wasted my life."

## 9. Include Everyone in Ministry.

God desires for each person to build up the Body of Christ. When any one person doesn't fulfill his or her part, the Body is incomplete. The "priesthood of all believers" is the community of God's people. A church is not a building or a program, but people living in love for one another and demonstrating the love of God to the world. This is why Jesus told us to love one another as He loved us.

A cell has no room for spectators. Members who don't fully participate in the life of the Body are also not fully plugged into the life source. For example, Samantha and Peggy are members of the same cell who came to know the Lord at the same time. Both are from broken families and had many hurts expressed through bitterness. After about eight months in their cell, their leader asked each of them to care for a new believer. Peggy accepted, but Samantha refused and said that she had not overcome her own problems. One year later, Peggy was growing by leaps and bounds, while Samantha was struggling with her same issues. When asked why, Peggy said, "Because I took the challenge to build up another person even through I was still very imperfect."

The church as Christ designed it has no pew-sitters. If you try to sit idly by and observe, others will nudge you, push you, pull you. You will be forced to change your ways either by participating or by leaving for another church.

## 10. Depend on the Supernatural God.

We are spiritual beings. Therefore, we are people of the supernatural and not just the natural. We must learn to operate in the supernatural, in the spiritual realm. The supernatural is the dimension of faith; the natural is the dimension of sight. We are told to live not by sight, but by faith (2 Corinthians 5:7).

This means we must have faith to believe God and to see with His eyes. Jerry had God's eyes for a new believer named Edward. When Edward first came to Shepherd Community, he had a bad temper and became especially angry when he felt dishonored. However, his life did not deserve honor. He was lazy, undisciplined and mean, and he could not hold a job. Even his parents had given up on him.

Through supernatural eyes, Jerry saw beneath the surface, prayed for Edward and spoke truth into his life. He and his cell saw a beautiful person inside, someone who needed help to surface. Through the love of the cell, Edward began to shock his family. He saw the dreams God had for his life. He became an effective minister. Now he is a cell leader who excels in helping other people who see themselves as failures.

Anyone can lead a cell meeting, but only God can touch someone's heart like this. A cell member can speak the truth in love, but only God can convict someone of unforgiveness or jealousy. A cell leader can visit and pray for a cell member in the hospital, yet only God can heal. God alone can restore marriages or turn selfishness into love. Only He can turn a prostitute into a church leader, or transform a youth on drugs into a worshipper.

This last condition can turn the tide of the other nine. If your cell group and church need an atmospheric change, begin with this value. Start with prayer and repentance.

Only God can turn death into life. He will touch those places that smell more like a dead skunk than a spring breeze. As your church adopts this culture of new values, a new way of living emerges. This culture creates a fresh atmosphere, and your church will become a magnet drawing people who need Jesus.

# 13

## The Key Is The Coach
by Jay Firebaugh

*After transitioning a church in Columbus, Ohio, Jay is now the assistant pastor/cell coordinator of Clearpoint Church in Houston, Texas. Clearpoint is a 10-year old cell church that anticipates over 80 adult and youth cells by the end of 2000.*

I'm a card-carrying coach for my son's T-ball team. For this honor, the National Youth Sports Coaches Association taught me things like, "Don't tell an injured player lying motionless on the field to get up and run it off." So I now press 7-year-old boys and girls to endure a 90-minute game on Saturdays, and in the process they sometimes catch the ball and run the bases in the right direction. They're learning.

Teams need the direction of a coach to get down the basics, to play well together and to win. A group of 7-year-olds without training, direction and encouragement will languish on the playing field. My goal as a T-ball coach is to help my team learn the essentials that will cause them to fall in love with baseball so they can enjoy it all their lives.

Frankly, coaching cell leaders isn't a whole lot different.

Our church's mission is to meet people where they are and to grow them into fully devoted followers of Jesus Christ. Through cells, we seek to accomplish this by encouraging our people to grow spiritually, know community, reach lost people and raise leaders. Coaches make sure that all the cells under him or her stay on track to accomplish these objectives.

Getting off track, unfortunately, is far too easy. We tend to get lazy about accountability relationships, or we fear transparency and hide behind an "everything's OK" mask. One of Satan's favorite tricks is to pull the group off balance by getting members to focus solely on, say, evangelism but ignore transparent relationships or spiritual growth. Balance in a cell is as important as balance on your car. I get my Michelin tires rotated and balanced every 6,000 miles because good tires can go bad otherwise.

Like the technician at my garage, a good coach keeps his cells in balance. They regularly watch over the condition of their cells, and they step in and correct any problem when they see imbalance or undue strain. That's why David Yonggi Cho, pastor of Yoido Full Gospel Church in Seoul, Korea — the world's largest church — says, "THE most important role in cell ministry is that of the section leader (a coach)."

I have discovered a key difference between cell church systems that work and those that don't: Strong cell systems include quality coaches who love cells and pass that joy along so cell leaders can effectively pastor five to fifteen people. Good coaches enable the system to work because they equip and support the shepherds, the cell leaders. They model, mentor and manage in a way that motivates cell leaders to stay at their task and produce Kingdom impact in the lives of their cell members.

## Modeling

Coaches model the ability to pastor people through cell groups. Coaches are raised up within the cell system, rather than appointed, because you can't train others to do what you are unable to do yourself. Don't merely decide that each of your elders will be a coach, or that someone will make a good coach because he or she is a godly person. Coaches must know from personal experience how to help people mature spiritually, experience community, extend themselves to their lost friends, and raise leaders within the context of cell life.

At East Side Grace Brethren Church, we are seeing anew just how critical modeling is. From the beginning, we have operated in a five-by-five cell model, meaning that each coach steps out of cell leadership to fully focus on the five cells he or she oversees. Each coach belongs to a cell but no longer leads a cell. We recently realized that a yearning to "get back to the action" of cell leading was frustrating some of our coaches. To meet their need, we are restructuring our coaches' duties so each will lead a cell and oversee one or two other cell leaders. Certainly, any coach who has been a proven cell leader understands the authority gained in being able to direct a cell leader on the basis of past experience.

This authority strengthens when coaches speak out of their current experience as well.

For example, I am a cell leader and a coach. I encourage my cell members to build relationships with people who don't know Jesus, so I earn the right to tell the cell leaders I coach to do the same. When I juggle my schedule to meet a cell member for breakfast, I gain the clout to push my cell leaders to do the same. A cell leader cannot readily dismiss the direction of a coach if that coach is following his or her own advice, and with success. That is the power of modeling. Coaches who aren't currently leading a cell, model for their leaders by how they live out cell life and cell evangelism. This is why we insist that every coach be part of a cell. Our coaches meet together regularly and love one another, but this isn't a cell. To effectively model the New Testament lifestyle to the leaders they oversee, coaches (as well as every pastor on staff) must live out a dedicated cell life, accountable in relationships and evangelism.

## Managing

Another of the coaches' responsibilities is managing the cell leaders under their care. In this capacity, they ensure that cell leaders practice the skills necessary to correctly lead a healthy, thriving cell.

Our coaches regularly attend the gatherings of their cell leaders, in part to show support for the group and their leader. Taking part in meetings and outreach events gives coaches a feel for the cells and for what is or isn't going on there. Visits put them in touch with their undershepherds' (cell leaders') members. These also are opportunities to observe the cell leaders "on the job," to find out what is and isn't working. A coach's feedback can correct a bad habit, such as a cell leader doing all the talking during the meeting or not beginning or ending the meeting on time. Maybe a leader isn't sharing the facilitation with an intern or isn't comfortable giving away portions of the meeting. A coach will recognize these and other shortfalls, as well as positive actions, and provide ongoing, fresh evaluations of the leaders' strengths and weaknesses.

The coach also is the vision caster for his or her leaders. My experience is that people stray from the vision if they aren't regularly reminded of it. Nehemiah discovered the same thing when, halfway through the rebuilding of Jerusalem's wall, the people needed reinvigorating to complete the task (Nehemiah 4:10). Nehemiah reminded the people of their vision, and they completed the project in a mind-boggling 52 days! This led Rick Warren, author of "The Purpose Driven Church," to conclude that people need to be reminded of the vision every 26 days, or roughly once a month.

Likewise, your cell leaders will lose track of their vision. Their cells will digress into self-focused clubs or denigrate into "nice" weekly meetings. Perhaps members will grow complacent about pushing each other toward spiritual maturity. These are the outcomes when a cell loses sight of evangelism, or when the cell gathering becomes a cognitive time to discuss scriptures and pray instead of a time to be transparent about what's really going on in members' lives. Good coaches know when cells and their leaders stray from the vision, and they work with the leaders to bring the cells back on track.

Administration and paperwork also fall under managing. Each of our cell leaders submits a weekly report to his or her coach. This report tells the coach what happened in the cell gathering that week (who was there, what they did, any special needs or concerns that arose). More importantly, though, the report highlights the leader's efforts to be involved in the lives of the cell members. A cell leader's greatest impact occurs not during the meeting but between the meetings, when he or she is connecting with members and facilitating "community happening." For example, are they talking with their members during the week, either in person or on the phone? Are they sharing mealtimes with members? Who are they praying for, and in what ways? Answers to these questions tell a coach how the leaders are doing.

## Mentoring

Perhaps the most critical element of coaching is mentoring the cell leaders. Coaches model what they want the cell leader to copy, and manage them so they are technically doing things right. But if coaches fail to do all this in a relational way, they miss the point of a cell church — "relationships," not "programs."

Cell leaders will copy their coach's example. If coaches only manage, they will produce a bunch of cell leaders who manage but don't pastor. To produce cell leaders who pastor their people, coaches must pastor their cell leaders. This means being intimately involved in their lives, not discussing only the practical aspects of their leadership. Coaches must care enough about their leaders' lives to ask how the marriage is going. How much time are they spending with their kids? What's going on with their job? How's their personal walk of faith? Their quiet time with the Lord?

This deep level of relationship naturally occurs when a coach oversees cell leaders they have helped raise up from within their own cell. They already are involved in each other's lives on a personal, pastoral level, and this continues with the addition of the managing and modeling aspects. Whether a cell leader is a product of his or her coach's cell, or whether the coach inherited this leader along the way, the coach must care for this leader on both a personal and a leadership performance level.

## Coaching Wisdom

Tom Landry, former coach of the Dallas Cowboys, said, "A coach is someone who makes people do what they don't want to do in order to achieve what they've always wanted to achieve." Cell coaches can't make a cell leader do something, any more than cell leaders can make the people in their cells grow spiritually. But the coaches' primary tool of motivating cell leaders to success is their influence through modeling, managing and mentoring.

Cell coaches have the vision. They've proven themselves as knowing how to pastor people. Through cell coaching, they expand their kingdom impact beyond their personal cell to include multiple cells, and then beyond that to a successful cell system. This system is part of a church that is about God's Kingdom business of impacting the world for Christ — people getting saved and discipled, leaders being raised up and equipped, Christians living out "one-anothering" in a way that makes the world around them wake up and take notice.

# 14

## Writing Great Cell Agendas
by Jim Egli

Watch a bird in flight, and you will notice that the two wings do not flap randomly; they are in perfect sync with one another. The cell church often is called a "two-winged" church, able to reach new heights because of the connection of its large-group and small-group wings. Just as in the early church, a synergy combines the dynamic of corporate gatherings and the intimate sharing of home groups (Acts 2:42-47).

What does it mean for your large-group and small-group wings to move in harmony with each other? Most cell churches create this synergy in part by dovetailing their cell agendas to their Sunday sermon themes. (For example, seven of the eight major cell churches researched by Joel Comiskey for *Home Cell Group Explosion* tie their cell themes to the Sunday messages.)

Corresponding your cell agendas to your sermon themes is not difficult, but a few important things really make it work. If you write dynamic cell agendas tied to your Sunday messages, your two-winged church can soar to new heights.

### What Not To Do

The cell groups are to follow the same theme and scripture as the Sunday message, but they are NOT to discuss the sermon. Your goal is to have people interact with God's Word, not with the sermon. Also, if the sermon itself is the reference point, visitors and those who missed the celebration service will feel left out.

When you write questions for the cell agendas, do NOT include questions that assume previous Bible knowledge. Focus on the plain meaning of the passage and its application. I remember leading a cell group with two brand new Christians in it. I asked how the message of the passage was exemplified in incidences from Jesus' own life. While it created lively discussion, the new believers sat silent, intimidated by others' Bible knowledge. Unfortunately, they did not return to the next week's cell gathering. Cell groups are different from Sunday school classes. The focus is on life application of the Word, not knowledge of the Word. Focus your questions on the simple, powerful message of the Bible passage and on how we need to respond to God.

Also, do NOT use a long passage. Pastor Dion Robert oversees one of the most dynamic cell churches in the world, in the Ivory Coast. His cell groups focus on just one verse each week. I don't restrict cell agendas quite that much, but the lesson remains: Stay focused. It is all right for cell leaders to occasionally deviate from the given agenda, but this should be the exception rather than the rule.

## Establish A Simple System

Writing cell agendas doesn't take a lot of time, but it does require a simple system. The first step in creating this system is deciding who should write the agendas. Many senior pastors write their own because the agendas are crucial to the life of their church. Other pastors find that they are not talented at crafting questions, so they delegate it to someone more gifted in this area.

The person writing the cell agendas needs the message theme a few days ahead of time so the cell leaders can receive the agendas the day of the sermon. Don't worry if the sermon changes at the last minute; the agenda will still be of valuable and can still be usable.

If possible, distribute the agenda to cell leaders in multiple ways. For example, we have mailboxes for the cell leaders and the agendas go in those boxes each week. But they are also sent via Email to those who have electronic mail accounts. That way, some who missed Sunday service or forgot to check their box get the agenda in a timely way.

For maximum life-change, follow a sermon topic for four to six weeks. This allows God's Word to soak in and take root in cell members as they hear the Word and discuss related issues over a period of weeks.

## Write Powerful Agendas

At the top of the agenda clearly put the week, the theme and the scripture. To illustrate a typical cell agenda here, we will use:

*Week of January 1 — "New Beginnings," Philippians 3:12-14*

The agenda should then follow the standard four W's:

### Welcome.

Include one or two icebreaker suggestions. These can follow the scripture theme or be related to the time of year. Icebreakers should be easy to answer and not consume much time. For our example you could put:

- *What is one thing God did for you last year?*
- *What is one goal you have for the year ahead?*
- *What is one thing you want God to do for you in the New Year?*

### Worship.

You don't have to include worship suggestions, but you can. Usually someone other than the cell leader leads worship. Remember that cells should use songs that are easy to sing and that are used by your church on Sundays.

### Word.

This is the heart of your agenda. State the objective of the Word time in the agenda. For our example you could write:

*Objective: Cell members will identify the things God is calling them to leave behind and bring these things to Him in prayer as they reach out to the new things Christ has in store for them.*

The most common error in cell agendas is including too many discussion questions. Most cell leaders feel obligated to cover all the questions you include. A good Word time has only three or four questions. If cell leaders try to cover more than that, the extroverts in the group will dominate the meeting. By using fewer questions and sitting on them, everyone is drawn in and interacts with the passage. This is crucial because introverts often have more profound answers. (They are actually thinking about the questions!)

Questions should focus on the main meaning of the passage and its application. Here are four questions that can be used repeatedly with some variation:
- *What stands out to you in this passage?*
- *What seems to be the main point of this passage?*
- *Can you illustrate this truth from an experience in your life?*
- *What is God saying to you right now?*

For our sample passage of Philippians 3:12-14, you could use the suggestions below in an agenda:
- *Have someone read Philippians 3:12-14.*
- *Ask: "What stands out to you in this passage?"*
- *Ask: "What is something that you gave up to follow Christ?" Note that some people give up obvious and ugly sins to follow Christ, but others like Paul have to give up things like religious legalism and self-righteousness.*
- *Discuss: "What are some obstacles that hold Christians like us from going on with God today?"*
- *Move into smaller groups with three or four men or women in each group to share and pray together around this question: "What is God asking you to leave behind and what is God calling you to reach for in the year ahead?"*

### Works.

This final part of the meeting focuses on outreach. If this is consistently squeezed out of your meetings, move it before the Word time for four weeks straight. It is helpful in the Works time to use a tool like TOUCH's "Blessing List" to keep cell members focused on praying for and loving their lost friends, co-workers and neighbors. We encourage the cells in our church to pray for the neighborhood of the home they meet in that week. Give practical suggestions like this in the Works portion of the agenda. Frequently suggest that they plan parties and cookouts and invite these people to attend. Also, highlight upcoming churchwide harvest events to mobilize the cells to pray for and invite unbelievers. For a January agenda on Philippians 3:12-14, you could use suggestions like these:
- *What obstacles are keeping you from being more effective in evangelism? How can those obstacles be left behind as you reach for all God has for you in the year ahead?*
- *Have your cell discuss the following questions in pairs and pray*

*together: Who is one person you want to see come to Christ in the year ahead? What obstacles are keeping that person from Christ? Take time to bring that person to God in prayer. Ask for the obstacles that you have named to be removed. Invite the Holy Spirit to reveal to that person their need and the love and power of Jesus.*

I highly recommend you dovetail your cell agendas to your Sunday sermon themes. If you have begun to do this, the suggestions above may make your agendas even more powerful. By dynamically uniting Sunday messages and application in the cells, your two-winged church can soar.

# Help! I'm A Cell Leader

# Section 5

# 15

# Seven Barriers To Growth
by Ralph W. Neighbour, Jr.

Ships sailing into unexplored waters are endangered by unseen barriers below the water's surface. Known and seen obstacles can be avoided; the dangerous ones are those who strike without warning. Many times the obstacles listed in this article are unseen until after the damage is done.

Consider these seven dangerous barriers to cell growth . . .

## 1. A Vision Not Caught by Every Cell Member

Church leaders transitioning a church must be sure the vision statement is in the hearts of all cell members. Traditional church members entering cell life may have existed for years without a vision statement. They often resist when goals and objectives are set to implement a clear vision.

The *Mission Charismatica Internacional* in Bogota, Colombia celebrated their fourteenth year with 10,465 cell groups. Their goal for January, 1998 is 30,000 cells. The only place left in the city that can house all the members is the 20,000 seat *el Campin de Bogota,* which they have leased Sundays for the next five years. The striking thing about this church is how the vision was imparted to every cell member.

Pastor Cesar Castellanos has shared a vision of planting cells in every area of Bogota and every community in Colombia. Cell leaders repeat the vision statement verbatim to all the members. As visitors gather outside the auditorium on Sundays, cell members nearby speak passionately about their part in making the vision come true. The level of commitment to the vision is as strong among the recently converted as in the heart of the pastor. It is a universal passion among all who belong to the church.

Church members who have not adopted the vision and participate with a self-seeking attitude become serious hidden barriers. There is a special bonding which takes place when a cell church has completely absorbed the vision of the set goals. Someone said, "I'd rather shoot at a goal and miss it than to shoot at nothing and hit it!" The vision must be simple enough to be accepted and implemented by every member of the body, or there will be no growth.

### How to Break this Barrier

When we seek God for His vision and receive it, it must be declared boldly. Too often the vision of the church is not clearly stated and repeated for everyone to embrace. Here is an example of a well written vision statement:

*Our Vision*
- *To establish integrated cell groups for outreach, discipleship and service which encompass the whole of our city.*
- *To be a church that equips every cell member, guiding each person to harvest the unreached.*
- *To establish cell group churches in other cities of our nation and overseas, sending out teams to reach neglected or responsive people groups.*

Such a Vision Statement must be printed in every bulletin, hung on every wall of the church facility and be written by each person from memory as a prerequisite for church membership. One South African pastor actually framed the Vision Statement and had families hang it on the wall in their homes.

## 2. Lack of Leadership

Pastor Castellanos often tells his people: "Our goal is not to recruit cell members, but to train leaders!" He begins a cell group with one person and encourages that cell leader to enlist twelve who will in turn be encouraged to form a cell of their own. His vision-casting is not just for his people to *belong* to a cell but to *lead* one. After only three months in cell life, every member is encouraged to attend a weekly cell leader's training class for three months. Thus, after only four to five months in a cell, 60% of the members are sponsoring a newly formed cell. They continue to attend the original cell, but are now called *leaders* instead of *members*. The multiplication is so rapid that this church multiplies three times in one year.

### How to Break this Barrier

Consider each cell member a potential leader and draw them into the vision. In Abidjan, Ivory Coast, Dion Robert develops three to four leaders out of every cell. In America, even the first generation of cells should multiply in seven to eight months. This means that every incoming cell member must be evaluated and mentored to lead a cell from the day they join.

Cells should live with a multiplication date set and declared to the group at its first meeting. Everyone should have a clear objective for the growth of the group through winning the lost to Christ. It will then be obvious that many cell members must accept the challenge to lead new cells.

## 3. Lack of Prayer

Pastor David Yonggi Cho has the largest cell church in the world, built upon an intensive prayer focus. Over two million visits are logged annually at the church's Prayer Mountain. On one occasion, Pastor Cho dismissed my interview in his office by saying, "I have an important appointment now. Thank you for coming." While I waited outside his office for a friend to pick me up, I saw no one enter for his next appointment. I finally asked Lydia Swain, his secretary, "Did Dr. Cho's appointment not arrive?" She smiled and said, "Each day at this time he goes to prayer. His appointment was with the Lord!"

This spirit of prayer must flow from the Senior Pastor to the entire church! Trite moments of prayer in a cell group are incapable of breaking the spirit of lethargy in a cell. Often growth is stifled because the presence and power of Christ does not overwhelm the group. It must always be remembered that each separate cell is the Body of Christ. Times of intensive communion with Him, with His Spirit manifested in the midst, will bring a new dimension to a cell. There is a heaven and earth difference in a cell that has experienced a *wipe-out* as He comes in all His glory during seasons of prayer!

### How to Break this Barrier

Many of the largest cell churches in the world begin the weekday schedule with prayer meetings. Members arrive at five or six o'clock in the morning to pray before going to their work. It is also common for a cell church to have a weekly half night of prayer, usually on a Friday evening. This may include intense prayer times for the church, the community, the nation and whatever else the Holy Spirit places in the hearts of the people.

In cells, intercession and warfare for the unconverted must become personal. During the *Share the Vision* time, the leader should display a large poster with the names of all unsaved *oikos* contacts. As this list is discussed, the Holy Spirit will create a prayer burden for those who have blind eyes and deaf ears. I have experienced cells that have prayed earnestly for these lost persons, or who have scheduled a special half-night of prayer to intercede for those on the list. During these times, the Spirit often shows the cell new ways to witness to these unbelievers. Many churches have also broken the barrier of barrenness by having cell groups prayer walk their neighborhoods.

## 4. Lack of Equipping

Tragically, the traditional church has not developed a systematic *boot camp* to prepare each Christian for ministry in God's army. The church staff members recruit appropriate people to operate the programs they supervise, but little thought is given to the urgent need to equip *every* believer for the work of ministry.

Cell churches must take seriously the need to equip every incoming cell member. Cell members will stagnate who are simply invited to *attend* cells, without clear equipping for service. In these cells, a tendency to navel gaze soon occurs, and members become obsessed with their own needs. They never learn to reach out to the lost. *The Year of Equipping* enables pastors and cell leaders to train and equip new members. My equipping track assists each cell member to examine and adopt a biblical values for their new lifestyle of evangelism and servanthood.

## How to Break this Barrier

Every cell member must be launched into *The Year of Equipping* by the second visit to a cell. Fastidious records of progress must be kept by the cell leader and the zone or church office. The accomplishments of those completing major portions of this *boot camp* training should be recognized by the whole Body at Sunday Celebrations.

After the basic training, further courses and seminars should be offered to develop skills for evangelizing, equipping and edifying. A cell church that grows trains within the life of the body rather than sending its members to study at a faraway school. A classic example of this is found in the Cornerstone Church in Virginia, pastored by Gerald Martin, where a full seminary structure has been added to their leadership training programs.

## 5. Lack of Deliverance

Incoming cell members may know they have a Heavenly Father and that their sins are forgiven, but they may enter the Kingdom with many strongholds. Areas of sins, bad habits, bitterness and unforgiveness often remain unchallenged for months or even years, because they do not understand the need for new believers to learn about satan, the accuser of the brethren, who goes about seeking whom he may devour.

The first priority for every new cell member must be deliverance. As Dion Robert says, *"You Westerners doubt that a Christian can have a demon. I want you to know a Christian can have anything he wants to have!"* Setting captives free is vital in a cell church. If this barrier is left in place, there will be many surprises as shipwrecked people and marriages unexpectedly appear."

## How to Break this Barrier

It is strongly recommended that *soul care* be provided through personal counseling and spiritual warfare retreats within one or two months of joining a cell group. When new members discover inner victory, God's refining fire will burn away lethargy in the meetings and inspire outreach to those controlled by satan. *Eglise Protestante Baptist Oeuvres et Mission* in Abidjan, Ivory Coast and the *Mission Charismatica Internacional* in Bogota, Colombia are examples of churches which have developed deliverance ministries for incoming cell members. Jim Egli has developed the *Encounter God* materials to help your church develop this ministry.

## 6. Lack of Community

Paul wrote in 1 Corinthians 12:21 that one part of the body cannot say to another part, *"I don't need you."* Philippians 2:4 reminds us that we should not look only to our own interests but also to the interests of the others. If cell members are limited to interacting with each other only once a week in a cell meeting, no bonding will occur. In such a group, the presence of Christ will not be evident, for this is not enough contact to create community and unity in heart and spirit.

Living in community is the very essence of the Body of Christ. We must be responsible *to* and *for* each other. Belonging to a basic Christian community is infinitely more than a weekly meeting. We are ligaments in Christ's body — responsible to support one another. It is imperative that a cell church have a regular schedule of retreats for cells and leadership, evangelism events and other activities that will establish community.

### How to Break this Barrier
Strong cell churches have *retreats* for cells and zones. Pastor Cesar Castellanos is currently building seven separate retreat centers around the edges of Bogota for the important weekends used for deliverance, soul care and cell leadership training events.

Cell leaders must be careful to create opportunities for cell members to have quality time together apart from the weekly meeting. This might involve a retreat every eight weeks, special evenings to celebrate someone's birthday or wedding anniversary, or having a cookout on a Saturday night, etc. Using the DISC profiles can be a tremendous tool to create sensitivity for one another. We must remember that the major ingredient required for developing community is time spent together.

## 7. Lack of Passion for the Lost

A cell group must see itself as a military platoon whose primary task is to kick down the gates of hell and snatch the lost from burning. A cell that is not leading the lost to Christ will fossilize! It is inconceivable that the Body of Christ does not have His heart and compassion for the lost.

Often, cell members ignore Jesus' command to share their faith with their *oikos* contacts. Cells should regularly see at least one new convert for every three members within six months. If there is no appeal for cell members to reach out and if the cell does not deliberately sponsor events to mix with the lost, there will be no harvest.

## How to Break this Barrier

The cell is a net that is cast into a sea of lost people. *Body life evangelism* represents the total cell community sharing in projects which involve unbelievers. Share groups and interest groups are excellent means of accomplishing this. Sometimes a need in an unbeliever's life can make it possible for the entire cell to witness. One example of this is a cell group in Houston who discovered one of their members had a leaky roof on his old house and had no funds to fix it. The cell group purchased shingles and roofed the entire house in one day. A great impact was made on the neighbors who saw this group of twelve swarming all over that roof and the front yard that a new cell was developed in that area.

# 16

# Six Habits of a Healthy Cell Leader
## What You Can Do to Bring Success and Ensure Growth in Your Cell
by Joel Comiskey

"How could this man multiply his cell group six times? He lacks the enthusiasm and bubbly excitement so necessary for small group multiplication." Then in my interview, Carl Everett, the man they call "Mr. Multiplication," confirmed my suspicion and told me that he was a very shy person. "How did you multiply your group so many times?" I inquired. "Prayer, prayer, and prayer," he asserted.

Carl and his wife, Gaynel, lead a cell at Bethany World Prayer Center in Louisiana. Their cell preparation includes fasting and prayer the day of the cell meeting. Before the meeting, they anoint the food, the sidewalks, the yard, every room in the house, even each seat to be used that night. They wait until after the meeting (during the refreshment time) to eat. The Everetts' example is not unusual at Bethany.

Is a day of fasting and prayer the only reason why some cell leaders succeed at evangelizing and giving birth to new groups while others stagnate? I visited eight prominent cell churches in search of the answer. More than 700 cell leaders completed my 29-question survey that explored such areas as the cell leader's training, social status, devotions, education, preparation of material, age, spiritual gifts and gender. This statistical analysis helped me discover common patterns across eight diverse cultures.

For example, I discovered that healthy cell leaders come in all shapes and sizes, and the anointing for successful cell leadership doesn't reside with a mysterious few. Some believe that healthy cell leaders are specially gifted, more educated and own more vibrant personalities than other leaders. Not so. The educated and uneducated, married and single, shy and outgoing, those gifted as teachers and those gifted as evangelists equally multiply their small groups.

However, several characteristics do distinguish successful cell leaders. These differentiating factors relate to what a person does as a part of his or her typical weekly lifestyle. It has nothing to do with personality, background or how long one has been a Christian. Instead, healthy cell leaders have incorporated certain habits into their life. You can join them.

## 1. Consistent Devotional Life

"I couldn't believe that the President of the United States wanted to meet with me! You better believe that I prepared for that special meeting. I wanted to honor him. I arrived at the White House hours early just to be ready. How awesome to be in the presence of the President!"

This scenario illustrates the excitement and anticipation of an important meeting. I never met with the President, but someone far greater desires to meet and talk with me and you every day — Jesus Christ. He's the King of kings and the Lord of lords.

The life of a healthy cell leader begins and ends with God. Only God can give success. My survey of cell leaders clearly showed that time spent with God is the single most important principle behind successful cell leadership. A cell leader filled with the power and love of Jesus Christ knows how to minister to a hurting member of the group, how to deal with the constant talker or how to wait for a reply to a question.

Why, then, don't cell leaders properly prioritize this time? There are at least three hindrances. First and foremost is drowsiness. We've all battled sleepiness during personal devotions. I'll never forget David Cho's advice about early morning devotions: "Get out of bed!" In bed, deep prayer can too easily become deep sleep. Instead, get up, wash your face, drink some coffee or go for a jog if necessary. Get the blood flowing.

Another impediment is our mind. How often I have approached the throne of God only to battle my thoughts — what that person thought of my comments last night, or when I should wash my car. "Your thoughts, Lord, not mine" is the battle of devotions. Ask Him to take over your thoughts in the "listening room."

Lack of time is another problem. Leave the fast-food mentality at McDonald's. In order to drink deeply from the Divine, you must spend time in deep meditation. As the Psalmist says, deep calls to deep (Psalm 42:7). Don't leave your devotional time without touching God, feeling the glow of His glory. This demands extended periods before God's throne. One or two short visits won't suffice.

## 2. Balanced Family Life

Everything smelled of success. The cells were multiplying. The church was growing and experiencing salvation and healing. But as staff members talked, it became evident that many cell leaders were suffering in their personal lives. They were busy every night of the week. One pastor asked, "Isn't it a contradiction to succeed in cell ministry but fail with our families?" Of course it is! In the life of a healthy cell leader, family is paramount. God desires to maximize our effectiveness as cell leaders, but not at the expense of our family life.

Cell ministry is a family affair and is meant to draw your family closer together. It's best to place your family inside your cell ministry. For example, your teenager can direct the children's cell or lead worship. Your child can lead the ice breaker. My wife, Celyce, and I minister together as a team in our cell. She plans the icebreaker and prepares the refreshments. I prepare the worship and the lesson. When she's leading the group, I care for our 2-year-old. Likewise, she covers for me when I'm ministering.

After cell meetings, we analyze together what happened. Once Celyce told me, "Joel, you should have been more gracious with Inez. I know she talked too much, but you could have handled it better." "That's not what I wanted to hear," I thought. But it's what I needed to hear. Our intimacy grows as we pastor our group together and openly discuss the details of each meeting, sharing our observations and learning together. This honest feedback also helps us mature as cell leaders.

## 3. Leadership Development

George Whitefield and John Wesley were contemporaries in seventeenth-century England. Both dedicated themselves to God's work in the same small group at Oxford University. Both were excellent in open-air preaching. Both witnessed thousands of conversions through their ministries. Yet John Wesley left behind a 100,000-member church, while George Whitefield could point to little tangible fruit toward the end of his ministry. Why? Wesley dedicated himself to training and releasing small-group leaders, while Whitefield was too busy preaching and doing the work of the ministry.

Yes, it's exciting to lead a cell group. But what will your group look like when you leave it in the hands of your current intern? Will it continue to meet or will it fold? Will you look back at your leadership with joy as you recall the cell groups that you left behind, or will you wonder how so much effort could result in so little?

We all know about the tyranny of the urgent. The cell lesson needs fine-tuning, someone must bring the refreshments, John needs a ride, and on and on the list goes. Cell leaders can be overwhelmed with worship choruses, ice-breakers, calls, visits, etc. Everything demands immediate attention. Or does it? In the midst of a fast-paced life, are there priorities? Can a cell leader confidently say, "This one thing I do"?

Yes. Successful cell leaders look beyond the urgency of the present to the importance of future daughter cells. Because of that, they spend priority time training new leaders. This passion to raise up new leadership drives successful cell leaders to spend quality time with potential leadership. As a result, common cell members become visionary leaders.

Leadership success in the cell church is clear: How many leaders have been spotted, trained, and deployed? Raising up future leaders is a Biblical way of life. Moses tutored Joshua, and Elijah trained Elisha. The Apostles were recruited and trained by Jesus. Barnabas discipled Paul, who in turn developed Timothy. The Lord has brought future leaders to your group. Are you developing them?

## 4. Inviting New People

The way to add future leaders to your group is to invite people to your cell — and keep inviting. Most cell leaders have heard the well-intentioned promises of those who failed to follow through. "Steve promised to come." "I planned dessert for four people who didn't show." Have you heard these comments before? Have you made them yourself? Welcome to cell leadership!

Experienced group leaders understand that you have to personally invite 25 people for 15 to say they will attend. Of those 15, eight to ten actually will show up. Of those, only five to seven will attend regularly after a month or so. Don't let rejection discourage you. Successful cell leaders don't depend on one or two verbal commitments. They continually invite new people.

One group at Bethany World Prayer Center faithfully met each week but experienced little growth. One member previously attended a group that had multiplied. After analyzing both groups, he said, "In the other cell group, we received a constant flow of visitors."

Another cell was celebrating the birth of a new group. The cell leader testified that the group went through a dry, difficult period. With only six people, the group did all of the "right things" to win non-Christians and receive visitors, but few visited and fewer stayed. Yet they kept on trying, praying and inviting until they broke through. Several visitors started attending and invited their friends. Because this cell resisted discouragement, the mix came together.

Cell leader, you personally must be vigilant about inviting new people. The right mix for your group is right around the corner. New blood in your cell will bring new life. Newcomers invigorate your group with their fresh insight. Keep inviting and don't give up.

## 5. Visitation

Luis Salas has a large, well-worn map hanging in the entryway of his Bogota apartment. This "war map" is overflowing with names of potential cell members. "I'm always dreaming and praying about new people to invite to my cell groups," he said. "All day long I think about them and eventually make personal contact with them."

In just 18 months, Luis multiplied his original cell to 250 cells because he goes after potential members. More importantly, he follows up with them after they visit. Some of them become cell members and then cell leaders.

If you want your cell to grow and multiply, one vital key to effective cell evangelism is immediate contact of visitors. When someone new attends your group, plan an immediate visit, send a card and/or pick up the telephone and call. The saying is true: "People don't care how much you know until they know how much you care."

## 6. Natural Evangelism

New members sense a freedom to share deeply in the warm atmosphere of an accepting, loving group. The "cell atmosphere" is the most effective way to expose non-Christians to the truth of the Gospel.

During one cell meeting, leader René Naranjo of Ecuador began a lesson on how Jesus cleared out the temple (John 2). Discussion flowed from the Jewish temple, to our own bodies as God's temple, to home cells as God's temple today. René guided the discussion when necessary, but the conversation flowed naturally and orderly. One couple said little, but they were asked to share their thoughts. This couple lacked a personal relationship with Jesus Christ, yet no one pounced on them with the Good News. They felt liberty to express themselves. René closed the cell by asking those who wanted to receive Jesus Christ to pray a simple prayer with him and visit with him after the meeting concluded.

In the last six months, René Naranjo has planted three daughter cells. He personally supervises these new cells and disciples the leaders. In his cell group, non-Christians feel comfortable to express their opinions, as he graciously points them to the Savior.

Are you targeting non-Christians in your group and including them in the lesson? Cell evangelism is not a programmatic, canned approach. Rather, it's a personal process of sharing Good News about forgiveness of sin and new life in Jesus. Because of the intimate, caring atmosphere of small groups, evangelism happens naturally.

### A Parable of Three Gardeners

A man had a beautiful garden that yielded rich and abundant food. His neighbor saw it and planted his own garden in the spring, but he did nothing to it: no watering, cultivating or fertilizing. In the fall, his garden was devastated, overgrown with weeds and bearing no fruit. He initially concluded that gardening does not work. After more thought, he decided that the problem was bad soil or maybe that he lacked a "green thumb." Meanwhile, a third neighbor started a garden. Though his garden did not immediately yield as much as the first man's, he worked hard and continued learning. As he practiced new ideas year after year, his garden reaped an increasingly abundant harvest.

The truth of this parable is obvious. I traversed the globe to discover the secrets of small-group growth, and the same principles made the difference between cell growth and stagnation in every country, culture and church. Prayer, hard work and the steady application of proven principles set apart the successful cell group leaders. The insights outlined here will work for you if you are willing to pay the price. These habits require time and effort.

Successful cell leaders spend time seeking God's face and are dependent on Him for the direction of their group. They prepare themselves first and then turn their attention to the lesson. They pray diligently for their members as well as for non-Christian contacts. But successful cell leaders do not stop with prayer. They come down from the mountaintop and interact with real people, full of problems and pain. They pastor their cell members and visit them regularly. They invite new people, visit newcomers and evangelize naturally in their small groups. By developing these habits, any cell leader can lead a group to grow and multiply. That is God's heart and His Great Commission. How are you doing?

# 17

## Life Together
### The Experience of Biblical Relationships
by M. Scott Boren

*M. Scott Boren is the director of research and publications for TOUCH Outreach Ministries, Inc. He is an associate pastor at Hosanna Church in Houston, Texas, and is a TOUCH conference presenter.*

Support groups, care groups, life groups, recovery groups, prayer groups, self-help groups, cell groups. We live in the midst of a small-group craze. Name the group, you can join it. Forty percent of the American population participates in "a small group that meets regularly and provides care and support for those who participate in it," according to Robert Wuthnow, a Princeton University researcher. People are crying out for relationships!

I fit the image of the modern man looking for a place to call "mine." I recently moved into a new apartment with my bride, Shawna. This marks my seventeenth home in the last ten years. I have bought into the constant movement of our time. We search for the pot of gold — new job, more schooling, better town — at the elusive rainbow's end, but we never stop to view the rainbow itself. We move on just in time to miss the beauty of living in true relationships.

### House to House

Christians in the New Testament found a remedy for our displaced world: They found solace in the church. They made church attractive and real. They related to one another. To illustrate how they lived, Larry Kreider, pastor of DOVE Christian Fellowship International, retells T.L. Osborne's fictional conversation with Aquila in Ephesus:

"Good evening, Aquila. We understand you're a member of the church here. Could we come in and visit for a while?"

"Certainly. Come in."

"If you don't mind, we would like for you to tell us about the way the churches here in Asia Minor carry on their soul-winning program. We read that you have been a member of a church in Corinth and Rome, as well as this one here in Ephesus. You should be very qualified to tell us about evangelism in the New Testament Church. If you don't mind, we'd like to visit your church while we're here."

"Sit down, you're already in the church. It meets in my home."

"You don't have a church building?"

"What's a church building? No, I guess we don't."

"Tell me, what is your church doing to evangelize Ephesus? What are you doing to reach the city with the Gospel?"

"Oh, we already evangelized Ephesus. Every person in the city clearly understands the Gospel. We just visited every home in the city. That's the way the church in Jerusalem first evangelized. The disciples there evangelized the entire city of Jerusalem in a very short time. All the other churches in Asia Minor have followed that example."

Homes were the centerpiece of New Testament life. Acts 2:46 reads, "They broke bread in their homes . . ." They met from "house to house" in Acts 5:42 and 20:20. The homes of Jason in Thessalonica, Titus Justus and Stepphanas in Corinth, Philip in Caesarea, and Lydia and the jailer at Philippi illustrate the central role the home played in the early church.

Some blame the modern malady of the church on the fact that we do not use homes as a means of ministry and evangelism. While meeting in a home is a step in the right direction, this alone will not fix your church. Small groups meeting from house to house will not make the world take notice and ask, "Wow, how can I be a part?" The 40 percent of the population who gather regularly in small groups and the 60 percent who choose not to are not looking for another meeting to attend, even if it is in a home. They seek something real, something powerful, something that will change their lives.

God does not give us easy formulas such as, "Meet from house to house and your church will grow." The power of the New Testament church supercedes meeting in a home. It supercedes meeting anywhere. The New Testament does, however, give us a model and a definition for relationships. It tells us how to live with one another as the church to impact our relationship-hungry world.

## Family

We read in Acts about how the church initially experienced the touch of the Spirit in the Upper Room. This moment directly impacted all of Jerusalem and eventually the entire world. Yet before the 120 in the Upper Room were ready to receive the power of God, He had to prepare the community. Luke tells us in Acts 1:14 that they were constantly praying. They remained together in one place (Acts 2:1) until the day of Pentecost. After this, the Holy Spirit filled those who waited on Him together.

We learn from this story that the Spirit does not fill individuals but people who relate with one another before God. The Spirit of God looks for people who seek Him together, who are willing to join in life together to reach the world. He fills them and unites such people.

The New Testament calls this "family." We belong to the family of God, according to Ephesians 2:19. Jesus said that those who do the will of God are His family (Matthew 12:50). The center of the New Testament church family was the home, the place of hospitality. Hospitality became the model for the life of the church. Through the transparent relationships of the home, the first cell members matured naturally. Conversation with friends, meals with family, and serving each other in the house became the means for living the Gospel.

If we are God's family, we must relate as family. Obviously we cannot interact as family with 75 other people who meet once a week on Sunday. Nor can we expect to develop an atmosphere of family by meeting once a week in a home. For example, imagine that your earthly family has a mandatory dinner every Thursday night. You gather around the table, pray, eat and talk about the rest of your week. This is the only communication you have as a family unless there is a crisis. Would you call this family? If so, your standard for intimacy and commitment is not very high!

Yet cell groups are described by many as a 90-minute Wednesday night meeting for prayer and Bible study. Meeting once a week is a step in the right direction but insufficient to develop biblical relationships. When we limit ourselves to a meeting, we miss the experience of hospitality. We miss the touch of friends available  only in the mundane parts of life: meals, working together, serving one another, long talks over coffee and playing board games until two in the morning.

The first time I experienced family in the body of Christ, I was heading a group of small-group leaders in college. I had no idea what God was doing. As I drove to our weekly meeting, God told me not to say a thing and to let the group set the agenda. As we talked, one student shared how she had been violated as a teen and that she was experiencing some healing. Later it came out that another young woman in the group had a similar experience. From this unplanned sharing of life birthed a family of countless phone calls, late talks over Coke and pizza, overnight retreats and ministry. God blessed us with the very simple miracle of family.

Most people in your group have no idea how to live as a family. This is Satan's scheme because he seeks to divide and conquer. Bad father figures, broken marriages and sibling rivalries are the norm. Satan wants to continue this pattern in your group. But people long for a touch, a hug, a phone call. You probably yearn for it too. Your cell can be a place to call home, where people feel welcomed and where Satan's loneliness is left at the door.

### Power

God poured out His Spirit in the context of family. Acts 1:8 says, "But you will receive power when the Holy Spirit comes upon you . . ." The early church stood out, and everyone in town knew when Jesus' church arrived. The people of God were marked by the presence of God. Some even accused them of being drunk! The church demonstrated His presence through signs and wonders, and saw the unbelievable happen as they continued the ministry of Jesus in His name. Peter and John healed the crippled beggar; Philip cast out demons and healed paralytics; Paul and Silas escaped from prison; Steven preached with power; 5,000 people confessed Christ as Lord; the church grew; and they remained in Christ for the long-haul.

Most of us have never seen God move like this. You might even think, "It was good for Peter and Paul, but God cannot do that through me." Or, "God only uses special people like a pastor or an evangelist." Well, you are special! Peter was a simple fisherman before Jesus chose him, and look what happened. Who were Philip or Steven or Lydia before God moved through them?

You can see God touch people miraculously, but your experience probably will not look like Peter's. Your story will resemble those of Mark's mother (who owned a home where the church met), Pricilla and Aquila, Lydia, Philemon or Nympha. We know little of these people except that they were faithful enough to be named in the Word of God. These were a few of the hundreds who prayed, ministered and labored behind the scenes.

In fact, the power of God probably will move through you and me differently than we think. Most believers will never reproduce what happens in a large crusade or on television. Some don't want to. But we can pray together for God to work. We don't need one man to do all the praying. Cell groups must learn that the power of God moves through relationships. If someone needs God's touch, the family is the means for that touch. In the normal ad hoc parts of life, two or three can gather in His name and minister to one another. We can do this as friends and become united.

After college, I asked God to move in the cell group I was leading. I did not know what I was doing. The group had no formal training. We just started seeking God. We grew close to people with deep needs — Don had cancer and had been hurt by the church, Sharon needed Jesus and healing from a recent divorce, and Jim struggled with sexual sin. We could not pray from a distance, with token requests and a closing prayer. We were too close and the needs were too great.

Seek God together for the impossible and watch Him work! When you start praying for deep needs of friends in the cell, your heart will break for them. You will stay up all night praying. You are no longer praying for an anonymous request or for the need of an acquaintance. You are now personally involved, and if God does not answer it affects you too. You will see miracles up close and personal and know that God is present. Your faith will grow, but even more your commitment to one another will multiply like weeds in the spring. And so will those asking you what is so different about your group.

## Purpose

Acts 2:42-47 tells us about the relationships in the first church: "Every day they continued to meet together in the temple courts. They broke bread in their homes and ate together with glad and sincere hearts, praising God and enjoying the favor of all the people. And the Lord added to their number daily those who were being saved."

Jesus says in Acts 1:8, "But you will receive power when the Holy Spirit comes on you: and you will use this power to minister to one another, develop deeper community and keep it to yourselves." No! He says "… and you will be my witnesses in Jerusalem, and in all Judea and Samaria, and to the ends of the earth."

With great sincerity some have said: "We cannot reach out to others. We are just getting to know one another. Our group is starting to jell and become a family."

C.T. Stud, a famous missionary to Africa, once said, "I do not wish to live 'neath sound of church or chapel bell; I want to run a rescue shop within a yard of hell." Does this describe your group? Is your cell group a rescue shop for your friends, family and others who are living a life of hell and are headed there for eternity?

Many groups claim to have deep relational bonds but miss the opportunity to run a rescue mission for the lost. Biblical relationships are fostered in a rescue shop. Jesus calls His disciples to lose their lives in order to gain it. Acts tells us how ordinary people took the message beyond Jerusalem to Samaria and to the uttermost parts of the earth. Biblical relationships have a purpose: to rescue the captives.

One of my best friends is Quan Hoang, my first cell leader. We prayed, praised and fasted together. We ministered to our cell members and stuck together through success and failure. We reached out to seeking friends and grew our group together. We fought together in the trenches. While walking in our purpose, we created a deep friendship.

You and your group are in the middle of a war. Your cell group is an army unit. When you wage war against the enemy to rescue the captives, you build bonds with your "army buddies." You learn to love one another in weakness, to fight together, to depend on each other. You discover the purpose of biblical friendships.

When you combine the element of being "army buddies" in the battle with the movement of the Spirit amid the group and the hospitality of family, your group will shine. People will gaze in wonder at your love for one another. Your life together will be real and much more than a weekly meeting in homes. You will have something worth their time and energy.

In the New Testament world, Aquila gave his home church much more than a house. He gave them experiences where they could encounter God and one another. Our world searches for this same kind of experience. Our call is to give it to them. There we will discover biblical relationships.

# 18

## The Body of Christ:
### Jesus is the REAL Cell Leader
by Ralph W. Neighbour, Jr.

Have you seen a TV program or movie that shows a lineup through a one-way mirror? Now imagine that you, as a cell leader, are watching a lineup of your cell group in such a manner. There they are: eight or 10 people, all with different needs and strengths. You have met with them long enough to know which ones are emotionally healthy and who is spiritually strong.

Look again. What (not whom) are you viewing? These dear ones are literally the body of Jesus Christ! 1 Corinthians 12 tells us they are all body parts. The Holy Spirit selected them (v. 13) and joined them together as hands, legs and even "inward parts."

Of course, you know which one overtalks and which one arrives late most of the time. But do you know *this* about them — every single one has the same degree of righteousness! Paul explains in Romans 3:22 that Christ is our only source of righteousness. When He indwells our lives, we receive all the righteousness we will ever have for all eternity.

I once sat in a Bible study led by Jackie Pullinger in the Old Walled City in Hong Kong. Those attending were former cutthroats and vagabonds who had recently accepted Jesus into their lives. While they were clean on the inside, their body odor revealed that they needed to bathe. Regardless, one of the seediest members of the group shared a profound insight with the others. A pastor friend looked over at me in disgust. He later asked Jackie, "Why in the world did you let that smelly bum share that spiritual insight?" Jackie scolded him: "Do you think because you went to seminary you have any more righteousness in you than he has in him? He has exactly as much righteousness right now as he will ever have, and if Christ wants to speak through him, that man has every right to be a channel for our Lord!"

Take another look at your cell group. Recognize they are a "basic Christian community," a fancy way of explaining they are joined to become the very body of Christ. His glorious Spirit lives and moves in them.

Sense the dynamics that take place as the icebreaker moves into worship and then into edification. Feel again the burden that arises as you share the vision and pray for unbelievers on your "Blessing List." Renew your awareness about Christ leading this group. You are only the facilitator!

1 Corinthians 14 speaks of the duties that each one is to perform (vs. 26). The term for "each one" in the Greek is *hekastos*, a word that depicts every person participating. In a cell group, there are not to be any "shy Janes" who passively observe the others. We are all expected to function as body members.

Body parts do not function independently. They are all directed by one source. The head of the body directs the hands, the eyes, the legs. None of these parts acts independently. There must be a central control, Jesus Christ, who induces the body to perform His ministry through them.

### The Christ Who Dwells in Me Greets the Christ Who Dwells in You

When Jesus lived on the earth, His Spirit occupied a body immaculately conceived. His life demonstrated the presence of God. He healed, He raised the dead, He cleansed the leper, He forgave the harlot. However, He could be at only one place at one time. His ministry was limited by His human body.

After Jesus arose from the dead, God gave Him a new body — one that exists all over the world, all the time. His new body provides the hands, feet and presence that penetrates all cultures everywhere. That new body is the cell group, the "basic Christian community."

Paul wrote in Colossians 1:26-27 of a great "mystery" that had been hidden for generations. He said, "I share this mystery: *Christ dwells in you!*" Think of what that means to your cell group: Every person in the cell has Christ living in him or her. He wants to cause the cell to function as His body, even as the body provided by the Father and Mary, His mother, gave Him opportunity to perform supernatural acts.

## The Main Factor in Making Your Cell Successful

The life force of a cell is Christ empowering it — Christ is in the midst, incarnating, indwelling it. He is the catalyst directing your cell how to grow and what to do. Christ must lead the cell. You are to serve the cell, but Christ must lead the cell. Beware of thinking too highly of yourself. You are a servant who facilitates the group so they can experience the life of Christ flowing into them for healing and restoration. Your cell members must also sense His presence guiding them into ministry to the unreached people around them.

I have often told cell leaders that they are not the group's "teacher." Nor is the assignment to be the primary caregiver and to solve every person's problems. Rather, their job is to create an environment where the presence of Christ is known, and where His life operates in the body members.

Here's a suggestion: Instead of trying to control the group during your next Edification Time, usher in the topic with a very brief review of the scriptural teaching presented by the pastor. Imagine as you speak that you are rolling a ball of introduction into the center of the circle. Then be quiet! Let the Holy Spirit guide what happens next.

I learned years ago to briefly introduce the topic to the group and then stare at the toe of my shoe. By doing so, I was indicated that I would no longer control what happens. After a period of silence, someone invariably speaks. He or she probably addresses me, but I deliberately do not establish eye contact. The group realizes that I have released them and will not guide the discussion. In that freedom, the body members begin to listen for the voice of the Head, Jesus, instead of the voice of the facilitator. What happens next can be awesome!

## Principles for Recognizing His Presence

The experienced cell leader is sensitive to the activity of the Holy Spirit as Christ guides the group. The leader knows that His activity is taking place when these things occur:

## 1. Meditation.

The group thoughtfully considers the direction in which the Spirit is guiding the edification time. They know that a cell meeting frequently focuses on one or two members, becoming specific in ministry to them. I have seen this scores of times. As a cell leader, I think, "Lord, I see that we are meeting tonight particularly because You want us to minister to Audrey as she agonizes over her recent divorce."

## 2. Transparency.

Usually the edification time begins with general statements by a few of the members. Others may still be thinking. I am sensitive to who is not speaking. At an appropriate time, I may say with a smile to a silent member, "And now — a word from Mary!" I try to help every (*hekastos*) person in the group to share. By the time one-third of the edification time transpires, I as the cell leader want to be sure each person has participated.

## 3. Confession.

Learn to read body postures by observing the group. If a hand or hands cover all or part of a face, that may be a sign the person is approaching confession. Crossed arms and legs may denote withdrawal or discomfort with the discussion. When a cell member shares deeply and perhaps makes an honest confession, the dynamic of the session takes a new direction. Christ has spoken in a special way to this person.

## 4. Compassion.

As the cell leader, I must now reinforce the group by confirming the person who is sharing deeply. Voice tone and repeating what has been shared is important: "Jim, I hear you saying that you have never been able to forgive your father for the cruel way he has treated you. Some of us have been there. We understand!"

## 5. Edification.

No issue is so deep that Christ cannot bring victory. When the group senses the activity of the Lord in one or more hearts, a time of silence is helpful so the members can reflect and hear what the Lord is saying. Remember that edification means that I hear your need, and then I hear Christ's voice, and then I share what He has given to me so you may be built up. Pausing to listen to Him in the edification time is very important!

## 6. Accountability.

Once the cell hears the clear words of the Spirit flowing through the sharing time, the cell leader needs to bring the issue to a conclusion. "Let's go around the group and share what each one of us has learned from this session. Perhaps some of us would like the group to know where we can focus our prayer about where we go from here." I recall one man saying, "Pray that when I pass by a newsstand in a strange city I will not be tempted to buy pornography."

## 7. Joy.

Many years ago, our cell was called to an emergency meeting by one of the members. With tears, the person confessed, "I have sinned against my Lord and against our life together as the Body of Christ." After the sharing, we promised to create a 24-hour prayer chain while this person travelled to a distant city where previous immorality had taken place. Many faxes and phone calls were sent by the cell to support this person. Just before our member flew back, we got a call: "I have found total victory from my sin while I have been here!" The cell greeted the member at the airport with a banner that read, "Well done, good and faithful servant!" We all rejoiced because one of the body members had been triumphant! When a cell finds joy at the conclusion of their lives together, Christ is in the midst in a special way.

### How to Tap into His Presence

The more time you spend in the "Listening Room" interceding for your cell members, the greater will be the awareness of Him when you meet with your group. As the cell gathered, I frequently sat with a deep sense of awe that we were about to assemble the hands, legs and other body parts of Christ, and that He would be revealing Himself in a special way that cannot be experienced by those who are not bonded into His glorious community. Intercessory prayer for one another is the secret of tapping into His presence.

## Be a Witness!

Once a cell discovers the active work of Jesus within them, the cell is never the same. It moves to a new dimension that shakes all their value systems. But that is not enough! It is evident from reading the four gospels that Jesus was ceaselessly active in reaching out to the lost. Indeed, He said He had come "to seek and to save those who are lost!" How, then, can a cell group *possibly* think they are pleasing to the Lord if they are not targeting a group of unbelievers and using their cell as a witness to draw others to Him?

1 Corinthians 14:24-25 makes it clear that the greatest tool of evangelism a cell group possesses is their meeting together with observers who are "unbelievers or ungifted ones." When Christ's presence is powerfully manifested in a special way in a cell meeting, unbelievers are awed by His evident presence and exclaim, "Wow! I have watched a lot of hocus pocus on religious TV, but in this room I really have met Christ. He is certainly among you!" And, says Paul, they will fall on their faces and be saved.

The full evidence that Christ is in your midst takes place when the unbeliever is also in your midst and finds Him in you!

# 19

## Get a Strategy
### Prayer and Planning are the Keys to Growth
by Randall G. Neighbour

As I travel around the country, the successful cell groups I visit live out a solid plan of action for growth. Cell members tell me that each one of them is a vital part of God's team because decisions are made as a group. The cell group regularly discusses its goals. Accountability is high. They see friends, family and co-workers come to Christ, and leaders are raised up from within the group. Everyone is on board, and the air is charged with cell life excitement.

We recently set aside two days for strategic planning at TOUCH Outreach Ministries, and I realized a cell group could do the same thing to achieve new results in cell life. Your group probably could benefit from a strategic planning and prayer session. Use the following information to form a weekend event, or tear apart the pieces and set aside planning time during your upcoming meetings.

### Pre-session Work

- Ask an "outsider" — your pastor, coach or supervisor — to facilitate the session(s). He or she knows the vision of the church, and is vitally interested in your group.
- If you can pull it off, take the cell away for a weekend to a retreat center or another remote location. If your cell is intergenerational and the children stay in your meetings the whole time, invite those 11 years and older to join you. Ask family, friends or other cells to care for younger children.
- Ask someone in your cell to plan the meals for the weekend. Keep meals (and cleanup) simple and short so no one misses the planning sessions due to "kitchen duty."

• Borrow a paper flip chart and an easel so your facilitator can write down all your great plans and post the sheets around the room for easy viewing. Take lots of colored markers and some way to hang the pages on the wall.

## The Big Event

Eat dinner together Friday evening, and then take some time to fellowship. Involve everyone in charades or another group game. Have some fun! End the evening with a time of prayer.

Start Saturday with an early morning breakfast, and have everyone clean up. See how quickly you can finish.

Post your church's vision and mission statements on a wall. Everything you do in this time must fit within these statements. Now you're ready to begin.

1. Pray. Open yourselves up to the Holy Spirit's guidance and cast off any ideas that are not from God. Christians often take on Kingdom tasks that belong to someone else. Seek only God's vision for your cell.

2. State and list your assumptions. Have your facilitator write each of these questions at the top of a separate clean sheet of paper:
   • What do we want to achieve this weekend?
   • What do we want to preserve in our cell?
   • What do we want to avoid as we plan for the future?
This creates ground rules for the session.

3. Answer the following as a group, and use the flip chart to record your answers:
   • What have been our successes? (recent past)
   • What have been our failures? (recent past)
   • What are our strengths? (present)
   • What are our weaknesses? (present)
   • What are our opportunities? (future)
   • What are our threats? (future)
This helps your group see the big picture and sets the stage for change.

4. Type the questions in this section and make a simple handout. Give each person a copy, and ask him or her to rate each question on a scale of 0 to 5 (0 is weak and 5 is strong). The facilitator jots down each number on the flip chart, and then figures the average for each question.

- I pray daily for my fellow cell members, the lost and my spiritual leadership.
- I spend time with lost people every week in an effort to show them Jesus through my lifestyle and actions.
- I have led someone to Christ in the last six months, and I'm showing that person how to do the same thing.
- I spend time with other cell members each week, either doing something fun or eating together.
- I am working through my church's equipping track for personal growth.
- I invest time in an accountability relationship with another cell member, and we now meet regularly.
- I have leadership potential, and I'm willing to pastor others when my group is ready to multiply and needs a new cell leader.

This identifies the common strengths and weaknesses of the group. Based on averages, determine the group's strongest and weakest areas. Discuss your findings and ask this question: "What must change to help our cell reach the lost and multiply its leadership base?"

5. Open up the time for confession, and surrender to God's call for His people.

6. Create a plan for the future. Pass out copies of monthly calendars for the next six months. Brainstorm and build a list of possible actions that would move the group forward. The listed items might fix identified problems, add missing components, or improve what already is working. Once the list is complete, decide as a group which ideas are the most important and "doable" by the group. These then become your goals. (Try to set dates for when each goal should be achieved, and assign specific responsibilities.)

7. Decide as a group how many new believers your cell needs to reach before multiplication. How many invitations to the meeting

must be achieved to reach this goal? On average, a group extends six invitations for each visitor who shows up. How many invitations must each member extend every week to reach your goal?

## The Bottom Line

Strategic planning melds your group as a team and creates shared vision. The group emerges with a clear purpose and an "outward" focus. Add a follow-up meeting to discuss how the plan is working and whether it needs tweaking.

Your strategic plan is your battle plan. We are at war, and Satan has fought hard to establish a reign of terror on earth. But we have the power of Jesus Christ — and Basic Christian Community — to overthrow his kingdom. Winning the spiritual war, and bringing the world to Christ, requires a solid plan, teamwork and measurable results. We must be strategic and determined to set the captives free.

*Strategic Resources recently helped TOUCH initiate a strategic plan of action for our future. If your church or organization lacks a strategic plan, request information from this Christian organization. Contact Ron Ford at (760) 634-6976 or send him an email at ronford@earthlink.net.*

# 20

## Time Bombs that Kill a Cell
### by Rev. Gwynn Lewis

**Too Many People in a Cell.**
The object is to multiply cells, not add people. A group will only grow to a certain point, depending on the size of the house. It can be exciting to have a group of 25 in the beginning, but the excitement will dry up. The group will stagnate and die. Real life comes from multiplying cells. When ten or more people gather together, the dynamic changes and intimacy is lost. It would be more productive to multiply this group into two groups of five. Always leave room for growth!

**Everyone is too comfortable.**
The "us four, no more" syndrome will stifle growth. As comfort levels rise, lethargy moves in. The comfy atmosphere will keep your cell from reaching out to the lost, hearing from God, and ministering to others if it involves walking on the edge or making waves. Don't confuse comfort with safety. Cell members need confidentiality and God's love for open and honest ministry. Separate the security of the cell from the non-productive comfort that will keep your members from reaching out to a hurting world.

**The cell meeting turns into a little celebration service.**
It's impossible to duplicate the dynamic of a big group in a small group. Don't try. The celebration format is centered around highly trained leader/teacher/musician types. If you do, cell members will become spectators instead of participants. Being small gains the advantages of open sharing, input, and group ownership.

### The vision is not reinforced.

If you don't carry the vision of servanthood and evangelism to your cell members every week, they will quickly form new reasons to meet together. Among your other responsibilities, you must be a coach and a cheerleader for your cell. Reinforce the vision of reaching out through testimonies, praise reports and group-planned outreach events.

### Failure to train leaders.

The growth of the cell movement is based on raising up leaders from within. The highest priority for the cell leader is to identify prospective interns and begin the mentoring process. When you minister to cell members and invest time in lifestyle evangelism, your interns should be there with you, growing and learning from personal experience.

### No ministry time in the cell meeting.

At least one third of the time of your weekly meeting must be open for God to move and for people to minister to each other. This is God's time — do not plan or structure it—wait for the Holy Spirit to move. Enter into God's power-time with the expectation that He is going to do something spectacular. Get out of His way and watch Him do extraordinary things through ordinary people. Remember, even pagans like to be prayed for . . . don't stop the ministry time when unbelievers are present. They will see the power of God first-hand, and say "surely God is among you!"

### Too much planning for cell meetings.

Most church leaders today are trained as program managers and the tendency is to develop yet another "small group program." The basic plan for a cell meeting is to have an ice breaker, a time of worship, time for God to minister through His people, and time to cast the vision of the cell through sharing and prayer concerning unreached *oikos* members.

### Too much reliance on human resources.

It is easier to plan everything out than to trust the Lord. The most powerful ministry and evangelistic tools available to us are spiritual gifts and basic Christian community.

### The people lose their vision.

People are capable of completely losing their vision in just a few weeks! This will lead to a lack of involvement or your cell will lose its primary focus. You must carry the vision and repeat the vision every week during cell to your members. Be the coach and the cheerleader for what Jesus has commissioned you to do. Rah, Rah, Rizm, Servanthood and Evangelism!

### Failure to find and train interns.

The heart and soul of a cell group movement is bringing up new leaders from within. If you focus on evangelism alone, you will reach the lost and leave them into a lonely spiritual life without mentorship. Focus on developing leaders rather than new believers, and include reaching the lost as part of their fundamental training. The highest priority for a cell leader is to identify a prospective intern and start training them. If you don't have at least one intern in your cell, you cannot multiply. BOOM!

### People's involvement in programs.

Involvement in church programs will siphon the energy for outreach from cell members. This is especially true of churches that are transitioning to cells. If a church is serious about being a cell church instead of a church with cells, you and your members must be free of other church obligations. Programs will keep you from dedicating the time and energy needed to develop a strong unbelieving *oikos*.

### The cell meets in the leader's home.

A cell will rarely multiply when this occurs. This sometimes leads to ownership and control problems, but more importantly, the leader should be the one to go out to the new cell with some of the members when it is time to multiply and leave his apprentice with the original group. Leaving your own home for cell life will cause large explosions with your family.

### Stagnation.

Never fall into a routine. Always look to the creativity of the members of the cell to provide new ideas. Newness brings a sense of novelty that attracts new people and keeps the old ones excited about being involved. God is a god of creation, He will continue creating, the Spirit will keep movement happening and Jesus Christ will supply the regeneration.

> *Day after day, in the temple courts and from house to house, they never stopped teaching and proclaiming the good news that Jesus is the Christ.* Acts 5:42

# 21

# Internal Exam

## How to Find the Person Who Has the Right Stuff to be an Intern

by Michael C. Mack

*Michael C. Mack is Small Groups Minister at Foothills Christian Church in Boise, Idaho. He is founder of the Small Group Network at smallgroups.com, an on-line ministry developed to provide training, support, and materials for small group leaders and churches. He is author of The Synergy Church and Introduction to Liberty. He acts as a consultant with individual churches who are starting or transitioning to a small group ministry model. He and his wife, Heidi, have two sons and two daughters.*

How do you find an intern? It is easiest to look at the outside of the person: skills, personality, education, ability to communicate. But while those may be of some help, they are not what is most critical. "Man looks at the outward appearance, but the Lord looks at the heart" (1 Samuel 16:7).

## What to Look For

The best intern is a FAT intern. There I go again, looking at the outward appearance! Not really. I do an internal exam to look for someone who is Faithful, Available and Teachable.

### Faithful

An intern is first of all a disciple. He has a growing, dependent relationship with God through Jesus. He has quiet time with the Lord regularly. He shows signs of maturity and a desire to keep growing. He is faithful in other areas of the Body: regularly participates in worship, consistent and reliable in other areas in which he has been involved, and consistent in cell attendance. He has a heart for God, God's people and people who do not yet know God.

### Available

My first intern was a guy named Jerry. Jerry had great potential. He had a Bible college degree, the gift of leadership, charisma, a wonderful ability to communicate and good looks to boot. But he had no time to be an intern. His work and a number of multilevel-marketing moonlighting jobs kept him busy all the time. He was not available, which made for a difficult, if not impossible, internship. Finally, he resigned as an intern, and we both breathed a sigh of relief.

Look for interns who have the heart of the first disciples, who left what they were already doing to follow Jesus. You can't expect someone to leave his job to be your intern, of course, but you can make sure he has the ability and willingness to follow.

Discipleship is sacrificial. It is costly. Jesus made that clear throughout the Gospels. But the rewards are sweet. Look for someone who is willing to throw his life into becoming a disciple-making cell leader.

### Teachable

The potential intern does not yet know it all and realizes it. She has a hunger to learn more about the Bible, facilitating a group, shepherding people and growing as a leader. The teachable intern is humble. She is willing to listen, model, practice, and give and receive evaluation. She accepts feedback, even in areas of weakness.

At this point you may be wondering whether such a person exists! Probably not, so you are looking for someone who is in the process of growing in these areas. No one is 100 percent faithful, or available 24 hours a day and seven days a week, or teachable all the time. Don't look for perfection. If that were required, you never would have made it as a leader — or as a child of God!

## How to Choose an Intern

"One of those days Jesus went out to a mountainside to pray, and spent the night praying to God. When morning came, he called his disciples to him and chose twelve of them, whom he also designated apostles" (Luke 6:12, 13).

As Jesus chose his interns (a.k.a. apostles), he did three important things. It would be wise for us to follow the Master's pattern.

## 1. Pray.

Prayer puts this important task in the right hands. It says to us and to God that He will do the choosing. As we pray, we seek where God is already at work, and then we join him in that work. Before Jesus chose the twelve apostles, he prayed all night. If Jesus found it necessary to pray before choosing his interns, perhaps we should too!

## 2. Call.

If you have carried out Step One, then this is God's calling, and you are His representative. Be sure you handle this as a calling, not just as recruiting a volunteer.

## 3. Designate.

What are you calling the intern to be? What did Jesus call his interns to be? The parallel passage in Mark 3 helps us out: "He appointed twelve — designating them apostles — that they might be with Him and that He might send them out to preach" (v. 14). The first part of the call was simply to be with Him. They would spend a lot of time with Jesus and have the opportunity to watch Him as He led. The second part of the call was to be sent. This is what internship is all about! It begins with time spent together in a mentoring, discipling relationship and grows to the point where the intern is sent out. The word apostle in the Greek means one who is sent, a messenger. An intern is one who is sent. He is like a missionary who prepares to be sent to multiply the ministry of the message of the Gospel. Be sure you designate the roles and responsibilities of a disciple and an apostle — one who follows and one who is sent.

That's the inside stuff of the Christian life — the stuff of internship.

# Children:
## Not the Church of Tomorrow

# Section 6

# 22

# Let the Little Children Come . . . (to my Cell?)

### by Lorna Jenkins

*Lorna Jenkins is an international speaker and consultant with TOUCH Ministries International on the subject of Intergenerational Cell Groups. She has worked with Dr. Ralph W. Neighbour, Jr. in the United States and at Faith Community Baptist Church, Singapore. Born in New Zealand, she is a pastor's wife. She has three grown children and several grandchildren. She holds the degree of Doctor of Ministry from Columbia International University. She has written various books and children's resource materials.*

When George phoned me again, I could tell he was excited. "Lorna, our pastor is curious about that idea you threw out at the end of our last conversation. Remember? You were talking about involving children in adult cell groups. I have to say I am still struggling with the idea, but our pastor says he has been thinking along those lines for some time. He wants you to come and visit with the leadership team."

Well, of course, I agreed. Two days later I was sitting with four church leaders in George's office.

Jeff, the senior pastor, began the conversation: "Lorna, George has been telling me some of the things you've been sharing with him, and we, as a church, are genuinely interested. We've been trying to incorporate our children into the cell church concept, but so far our efforts have been less than fruitful. In fact, my daughter tells me that it still seems much like Sunday School. Also, I was reading about a group in Canada where the children and the adults were in family groups, and it seemed to be working fine for them. But I'm not sure if it would work here."

" Well let's take a look at the concept," I said. "Several churches are experimenting with children's cells, and they certainly aren't bound to one particular format. I know of a church that included children as full members in its regular cell group meetings. They met together for about 30 minutes, and then separated for about 45 minutes to an hour. At the end, the two groups would come back together."

Ella broke in. "What age of children would come to such a

group?" she asked. "I think the little ones would find it very hard to sit still."

I smiled. "Little ones always find it hard to sit still. They're not built that way. But that doesn't mean they should be excluded. A cell group is like a family. If a young child is present, he can wander around to visit members of the group, sit by different people or get busy on an appropriate activity. The group will develop a tolerance for children they know and love. Small children can sleep in another room when they get tired. Of course if a child is distressed, he will tend to run to his parents."

"Who looks after the children when they separate off into another room?" asked George. Would a trained person from the children's ministry do this, or would the parents take turns?

"It defeats the purpose if you call in someone else outside the group to care for the children. The children read that as 'babysitting.' To be part of the cell group, they need to get to know the adults. But the adults don't want to miss the closeness developing amongst their peers. Therefore rotating the leadership of the sub-group is effective because no one is excluded from the adult group every time. This arrangement also blesses the children. They not only share time with all the adults in praise and worship, they get to know them individually as well."

"Some people just don't handle children well. In fact, I have to admit, I'm one of them," confessed Tim. "I don't even know what to say to a child. Would everyone have to take a turn?"

"You're right, Tim," I answered. "I find many people are very nervous about relating to children. Some of them absolutely back off, while others look forward to this interaction and even feel especially called to minister to children. No one should 'have to take a turn.' But, if given the chance, I've found that people who are inexperienced with children are surprised to discover how much they enjoy their company and friendship."

"What exactly do you do with the children in the cell groups?" asked Jeff. "We've got our cell groups running smoothly, and I wouldn't want to upset that by introducing the children. However, I do see advantages from a family point of view."

"That's a valid fear, Jeff," I said. "Children really don't change the nature of a cell group. They just broaden the concept. The basic elements still exit. The icebreaker, praise and worship, mutual prayer and ministry, vision casting, food and fellowship can all be done with the children present."

"While in separate groups, children can discuss the week's events from their younger point of view. Take, for example the message from Sunday's teaching. The children may have heard a different message than the adults, and they will have a different set of problems because they live in a different world. They need to talk these things through at their level and discover what God is saying to them. If God reveals areas needing growth, the group can pray for an effective plan of action and then remain accountable to one another as God begins to produce fruit within them."

"So you're saying that the children share their needs with their smaller group and join in ministry with the whole group as well. " George was nodding.

"Yes, but sometimes the adults will have needs they do not want to share before the children, and the children may have some needs they do not want to express to the whole group. It's good for children and adults to understand each other's lives and problems, but there are some things which are too personal for the open group. . . . By the way, if you include the children in the cell group, they will be subject to the same group agreement as all the other members of the group."

"You mean in the area of keeping confidences? Can you really trust children no to talk about what they hear?" asked Jeff.

"Not always," I sighed. "About to the level that you can trust adults. Remember not to laugh at them or scold them. The adults must assure the children that they are trustworthy listeners as well."

"I suppose when you put it that way, the risk is about even," replied Jeff. "The cell leader has to use discretion about what to discuss and when the children should leave."

"You know I've been a school teacher for a number of years long before I started working for the church," began Ella, "and I'm a bit worried that this whole approach with children may be too advanced for them. Are we expecting them to act like little adults? Children don't want to be too serious. They like to have fun."

"It's true that children do not like being solemn all the time, but they do like for adults to take them seriously. Once convicted by the Holy Spirit of their need for Jesus, I find that children are serious about following Him. They pursue answers to their problems very seriously. They are serious about developing relationships in their lives. And amazingly, as their understanding of praise and worship grows, they become serious about this as well.

"But the intergenerational cell group is not always supposed to be serious. Children provide a breath of fresh air, and they remind us of the trusting life God has called us to live. Then as the children spend time together, they share creative activities, initiate service projects, and most importantly, learn to pray for their friends, family, and the world."

"I can see real merit in having the children in the group during social activities," offered Tim. "At present, if we have a group picnic, the children feel shy and isolated because they barely know the adults in the group. "

"True Tim," I answered. "Also, you might plan one night just to have fun together. You could create a drama, put together a music group, or just play some games. You lear a lot from children in such a casual atmosphere, and it's a wonderful time for them to bring their friends."

"Don't you think every once in a while an adult night would be appropriate?" asked Ella. "I'm thinking it would be good, especially for those members of the group who do not have children."

"You could certainly do that," I said. "Children do not necessarily expect to be included in everything. However, you may be surprised how quickly the singles learn to enjoy the children. Often the children look up to an adult friend as a role model, thus both the singles and children are crucial to the group. Also you should tap into the resource of skills within the group. Someone might be able to help a child with his math when his parents lack that ability. Another may be a football expert. Children readily identify with older people who possess interests or skills which they are trying to develop.

"You know, children are also a powerful catalyst for evangelism. As they bring their friends to cell activities, the adults can befriend the new children's parents. The open arms of the group can win the entire family to the Lord. When a whole family enters a cell, the growth potential is tremendous."

"Well, just thinking structurally for a moment, how many children would you include in an intergenerational cell group, Lorna?" The pastor was jotting notes on a pad.

"If a cell group has up to fifteen adults, I would like to see no more than 8-10 children between the ages of 4-13 years in one cell group. Babies and toddlers are in a different category, though I wouldn't want the group to be dominated by the babies. Of course when the cell group multiplies, the children would go to the same new cell group as their parents."

"What about teens?" continued the pastor.

"Technically they should be part of an intergenerational cell group too," I answered. "However I've found that teens need to establish themselves amongst their own peers, and some churches create cell groups just for this purpose. Teens appreciate the freedom to grow without the looming shadow of their parents. On the other hand, youth have much to give and receive in an intergenerational setting. You can decide which arrangement best meets your particular needs."

"Lorna, we're going to be doing some serious planning and praying here about our children's ministry," said Jeff. "We'd like to be able to call on you as a resource person."

"Certainly. I'll be glad to help. Jeff, I believe that children's ministry is at the forefront of the spiritual battle in the world today. If we lose that battle, we could lose the next generation. But I don't believe we're going to lose this fight, for 'the battle belongs to the Lord.' He is raising up churches just like yours, who are placing children where they belong, right in the center of the Kingdom of God."

# 23

# Children Love Cells
## How to Have Successful Children's Cell Time
by Holly Allen

*Holly Allen teaches in the Education Department at Abilene Christian University and was the Director of Children's Ministries for a cell church in Abilene, Texas for four years. She is currently pursuing her doctorate in Christian Education from Talbot School of Theology.*

If you want to know the truth about something, ask the children. They will tell you. When I asked some of the children in a cell group what their special memories of children's cell time were, they said:

7-year-old: "I remember when Mr. Leonard (senior pastor) sat on the floor with us and listened to us."

4-year-old: "I like to be with the big kids and do what they do. They let me talk and everything."

15-year-old: "I remember when Jeff blindfolded us and led us around the furniture. He said that is the way God leads us, and we should trust Him."

9-year-old: "I remember when I was afraid to go to public school because I had been home-schooled. All the kids prayed for me."

When leaders in new cell churches hear these testimonies they ask: "We like the idea of children's cells, but how can we create children's cells that work? How can our children learn to pray for one another, love one another, minister to one another?"

## What is a Children's Cell?

A children's cell is "a small group of children bonded together around a leader for mutual care, prayer, questioning and discussion. Living their Christian life together, they reach out to serve others and to win other children to follow Jesus" (Lorna Jenkins). This cell (often called the Kid's Slot) is a sub-group of the family cell.

In actuality, children's cells function like adult cells. The goal of children's cells is to meet children's spiritual needs much as adult cells meet adults' spiritual needs. But most cells do not know how to create children's cells that do this. Intergenerational cells needed guidance with their children.

To facilitate the children's cell, each family cell should designate a children's cell coordinator. This person does not lead every children's meeting, but he or she gives oversight to the ministry to the children. Each week adult cell members take turns as the children's cell leader. Everyone in the cell should be able to love the children and lead them through simple activities and stories.

## A Children's Cell Format

Over the years, I have wrestled with what a children's cell looks like. I began writing children's cells guides to provide structure and direction for the various adults who lead the children's cell or Kid's Slot. Though the format for each cell guide varies somewhat, the common components include an icebreaker, prayer, Bible story, theme activities, sharing struggles and victories, listening, and regrouping with the adults.

### Ice breaker
The icebreaker is usually a simple, non-threatening question like, "What is your favorite ice cream?" Sometimes the question connects to the Bible story or biblical theme being emphasized that evening, such as, "What would be difficult about being raised in a king's palace?" (This icebreaker accompanies the story about Moses being raised in Pharaoh's house.)

Each child usually answers the ice-breaker, though it is not "required." Visitors are encouraged to answer but are given an easy "out" by saying, "Would you like to tell us your favorite zoo animal or would you like to pass?"

The children look forward to the icebreaker each week and expect it. Though the icebreaker time is light and easy, it can lead to deeper discussions and prayer. I remember when the story time was about Ananias and Sapphira, and the icebreaker was: Can you think of a time when you told a lie and got caught? I began the icebreaker by confessing a lie I told to my sixth grade teacher and how he found out and what happened to me.

The children were fascinated by my story and wanted to hear all the details and how it turned out. Two or three remembered specific lies (and consequences). A preschooler said there were monsters under his bed. One second grader said that she sometimes didn't tell the truth, and she was afraid that she was a really bad person. We prayed with her for forgiveness.

In this case, the icebreaker led to confession and a way to acknowledge and work through the sin and the fear.

## Prayer Time

This is a time for sharing victories and struggles. The children's cell coordinator keeps the prayer journal that is passed each week to the children's cell leader so that last week's prayer needs can be reviewed.

One week a tender-hearted child (Erin) asked the cell to pray for a girl at her school who was being bullied (Sara). The next week the other children asked how the week had gone for Sara. "Not very well," was the response. Another child suggested they pray for the main bully (Justin). They did. Every week for months the children prayed for Sara and Justin. Eventually Erin asked that they pray for her. She wanted to befriend Sara, not just pray for her. A few weeks later Erin asked that they pray that she might publicly defend Sara. Each week the current cell leader noticed the prayer need in the journal and each week the children prayed. Though Justin was still bullying Sara at the end of the school year, the whole children's cell realized the biggest change happened in Erin. She had learned to stand up with courage for a friend.

## Bible story

The children's cell should also include a Bible story. The children's cell guides I developed always include a synopsis of the Bible story, the scripture reference and directions for a fairly active way to tell the story. For example, the children pass around a heavy rock while the teacher tells the story of the Israelites as slaves in Egypt from Exodus 1. Sometimes a thumbs up, thumbs down script is included:

- *The spies went into the land as God had told them.* (thumbs up)
- *Ten spies said the land was too hard to take.* (thumbs down)
- *Two spies said the Lord would enable the Israelites to win.* (thumbs up)
- *The Israelites believed the ten spies.* (thumbs down)

A more active way is for the children to stand up or sit down instead of using their thumbs. The children's cell leader can decide how active the story telling needs to be.

There are a variety of creative ways to communicate the Bible stories. Sometimes a script for adult "actors" (parents or other adult cell members) is included. Other times the children are given art supplies to draw the story as it is told. Sometimes directions are given for helping the children enact the story. The goal is not only to communicate facts, but also to provide an opportunity for children to learn by interacting with adults and one another.

### Share personal insights

At this point, the children's cell leader is encouraged to share a time when God has worked powerfully in her own life. This is the time when the most significant things happens in the children's cell group. When the various adults who take turns leading the children's cell share what God has been doing in their lives, confess areas of weakness, and pray for God's guidance, the children see God is working in the Christians around them. They discover that the adults they know seek God in all they do. Basically, the children are privy to the "normal Christian life" as lived by the adults in their church.

Sometimes following the sharing, there is a time for "listening" to God, a time for making scripture real and usable or a time for asking for God's empowerment in overcoming sin or for healing.

### Regrouping with adults

When cell time is over, the children regroup with the adults for a few minutes to share something they did in their cell time. They might repeat the "Thumbs Up-Down" activity, re-enact the story or share food they have made. They might say the Ten Commandments or a memory verse or share an answered prayer. The cell guide offers one or two suggestions each week. This closure activity renders two important functions: first, it signals to the adults that the children's cell is over, therefore the adult cell needs to end soon. Second, the children get to share what they have been doing, helping them (and their parents) realize that these activities are important, not merely busywork.

## Meeting Children's Needs

Over the period of a school year, the children in a children's cell come to know each other well; they play together, pray together, praise together. They bond together. They begin to feel safe enough to confess needs and fears. They learn to pray for each other and minister to each other. They experience God's powerful work in their lives. They see that God is working today on the behalf of His people as He did for His people of old. They begin to realize that they are His people.

It isn't necessary for the children's cell guide to be followed exactly for children to see God; perhaps only a few of the suggestions on the cell guide will be completed. The purpose of the cell time for children is the same as it is for adults — to address their spiritual needs. Just like adults, children need a place to be accepted and loved, to share their needs and fears, to pray for others and to be prayed for, to forgive, to confess, to experience God. A children's cell can be that place.

# 24

## The Youngest Evangelist Speaks Out
### God is Using Little Ones to do Great Things
### When We Encourage Them
by Jessica Osborn, age 11

*Jessica Osborn is a member of New Community Fellowship, a cell church in Virginia Beach, VA. As a homeschooler, she loves to play hockey and is involved in gymnastics. She occupies her free time with friends and likes sleep-overs. Oh yes, she asked us to remind you that she loves her youth cell!*

My father pastors a cell church and I had some Christian friends at Church but I didn't have any Christian friends to hang out with in my own neighborhood. I wanted to start a youth cell in my neighborhood so my friends could get saved.

I asked my mom and dad if we could start a youth cell in our home. I hoped and prayed that they would say "yes." They said they would pray about it, and a couple of days later they said that I could.

First, we had to decide on what day we would have the cell meeting. We decided on Tuesday nights, because Monday is my father's leadership night and our family cell is on Wednesday nights, and on Friday my father takes my mom out and I baby sit. My Dad said, that because of his busy schedule, I would have to invite the kids. He also said that I would have to help mom get the house ready.

I asked my friends Mike and Stephanie if they would like to come to my home the next Tuesday for a youth cell. I explained that we would have a snack, play games, and have a Bible study. They said that it sounded like fun and they would come. They asked some of their friends if they would like to come too.

When Tuesday came I helped my mom get the house ready. I cleaned up and she made brownies. She asked me how many kids were coming and I didn't know! I was kind of scared and wondered if anybody would show up. Seven kids joined us and I was really excited. I think my Dad was surprised as well.

We played some really fun games and my Dad did a couple of

ice breakers so everybody could get to know each other. My friends ate all of my mom's brownies.

After everybody left I felt really happy that all my friends came. Before I went to bed I gave my dad a kiss and told him thanks for doing it for me.

The next day I asked my friends if they liked it and if they would come back again the next week. They all said that they would and promised to invite some of their friends.

The next week they all came back and brought friends. Within four weeks there were about 20 kids coming every Tuesday night! That was weeks ago. Now I don't have to remind the kids about youth cell. They just keep showing up at our house on Tuesday night.

A lot of neat things are happening in my friends lives. Many of my friends were smoking cigarettes and marijuana and drinking before they started coming to cell. But God is changing their lives. I pray that all my friends will get saved.

In cell one night, five of my friends got saved. Everybody was crying as we all held hands. My friends prayed to receive Christ. My dad told them that accepting Christ was just the beginning. It was the first step. Now they have to live their lives for Him. Most of my friends are Christians now and the others come to church with me on Sunday mornings.

A few weeks ago, we loaded up three van loads full of my friends and took them to church on Sunday morning. We all sat in the middle of the church on the front row. I think everybody wondered where all these teenagers came from. My friends all thought the church was really cool. (My Dad took us out for pizza afterwards).

Many of my friend's parents are divorced or don't get along very well. Some of my friends have been abused by family members. So they like to hang out at my house. My mom and dad always let my friends eat with us. And almost every weekend I have friends spend the night. My church has bought all of the kids in our cell Bibles for Christmas because most of the kids don't have one.

I'm happy that I started this youth cell. I now have Christian friends in my own neighborhood to hang out with. I know it's a lot of work for my mom and dad. I am very happy that they have helped me reach my friends for Christ.

I think that every Christian teenager that doesn't have Christian friends in their neighborhood should start a youth cell. I know that the kids will come and get saved. All you have to do is ask your mom and dad to let them come. Then, if they say yes, invite some of your friends, and have them invite some of their friends. Then pray for your friends to accept Christ. It's simple.

# The Rapidly Growing Youth Cell

# Section 7

# 25

## Entertainment Evangelism
### Winning the Battles, Losing the War
by Ted M. Stump

*Ted M. Stump is the founder and director of High Impact Ministries. He holds a Master of Divinity from Columbia Biblical Seminary. Ted's ministry experience includes study and travel with Dr. Ralph Neighbour, Jr., Josh McDowell, and evangelist John Guest. Ted serves as a national and international consultant to churches and youth organizations on developing and implementing Student-Led Cell Groups.*

We have produced a generation of youth that are consumers with the attitude of, "Hi, my name is Jimmy, What are ya' gonna gimme?" Our present methods of ministry reflect and breed this type of consumer.

I have recently resigned as youth minister of one of the fastest growing churches in the United States. It had at the center of its mission, "Entertainment." The strategy was to bring in the multitude and entertain them with quality music, drama, comedy, and non-threatening user friendly messages. It is even putting together a country & western service for those "Red Neck Jimmy's."

As the head of the youth ministry, I proceeded to offer the finest quality of entertainment to our youth. We had smoke, lasers, comedians, professional football and basketball players. We invited an Olympic pole-vaulter, Mr. America, Mr. Universe, and Mr. World. We took them swimming, fishing, skiing, surfing, and skating. We played broom ball, volleyball, fooseball, ping pong, wallball, and beach ball. After we got tired of following the bouncing ball, we would start over.

Then it happened; Jurassic Park came out and a group of Jimmy's got together and threatened to leave the youth group if we couldn't provide a live dinosaur. That was it. It finally happened — we couldn't keep up.

Every night when the smoke cleared, the bands went home and hundreds of youth filed out of the door. With tears in my eyes I asked myself what we had really accomplished. Sure, we had shared the gospel and the youth responded, but I knew a multitude went away hurting.

This form of ministry reminds me of a show on TV years ago. A man would spin as many plates as he could on top of poles. He would keep adding to the number of plates spinning until he had to re-spin the ones that were slowing down. One by one, each plate eventually crashed to the ground, prompting howls from the onlooking audience.

It's the same way with program-based youth ministries. We had a program for everything. When we finally had one program going well we would have to move on to another — only to return to the first to jump-start it. It is no different than the hectic pace of adding plates, running back and forth endlessly, knowing full well that the plates will eventually lose momentum and fall.

Perhaps entertainment worked in the 80's, but this generation lives in a society that devours its youth. Teenagers in the 90's face incredible challenges. Suicide remains the number two killer of youth today. In fact, it's up 400% in just the last ten years. Teen pregnancies and abortions continue to steadily increase and gang violence has impacted virtually every high school across the country. In addition, divorce has left many teens without a sense of acceptance or belonging.

If we think entertainment evangelism can help this generation of the walking wounded, we need to wake up. We, as ministers of youth, will never be able to compete with what comes out of Hollywood, but let me tell you something. Hollywood can never compete with what comes out of the Word of God and the power of the Holy Spirit that can transform an individual's life.

There is a powerful movement of the Holy Spirit around the world which has transcended denominational lines. It is the cell group church. I have spoken with countless youth pastors who have been prompted by the Holy Spirit to move towards a cell group youth model for their ministries. It is the answer to this generations needs.

Today's youth have been called the "baby busters" — children of baby boomers. They were given the name because they have been handed a world that is broken. God is raising up a structure that will help put back the pieces.

In future articles, we will deal with some specifics of youth cell groups: how to form them, curriculum, leadership, administration, training, and much more.

If you're spinning plates, don't give up hope — there's another way.

# 26

# Gathered in My Name
## How to Transition a Program-based Youth Ministry into a Relational, Student-led Cell Groups
### by Ted M. Stump

That night, six out of thirteen students shared how they had attempted or strongly considered committing suicide. The cell topic was depression and suicide. The leader was a sophomore in high school who had been leading cell groups for over a year. The students looked like your "normal" mix of kids, most involved in sports. One by one, they shared painful experiences in life that caused them to contemplate or attempt suicide. The whole room was brought to tears on several occasions due to the pain shared by their peers. The Holy Spirit lovingly ministered to this dear group of youth. The next day, the leader's mom shared how greatly impacted her son was by the testimony of his friends; he will never be the same.

There will never be enough "professional" youth workers to reach the multitudes of youth in our world, but there are enough students with a heart for their peers that if equipped could reach their peers.

Take a good look at your current youth ministry model. Are you running from one event or program to another? Have your ever sat down at the end of an event and asked yourself what did we really accomplish? Do you feel you must always do things a little bigger and better each time?

There is a movement happening all over America and around the world. God is restructuring His church into a relational cell-based ministry. This article will deal with how to transition an entertainment or program-based ministry into a relational student-led cell-based ministry.

So how do you make the leap from one model to another?

### Pray
Seek the mind of the Lord. Has he called you to a new work? Until you have God's peace to move on, stay on your knees.

If you view this as just another program or church growth principle, then you will give up on it when the next "hot idea" comes along.

### Evaluate
Take an honest look at your ministry. How is the Lord working in your midst? Are you producing disciples who will dedicate their whole life to His service? How do you invest your time, in programs or people? What are your strengths and weaknesses?

### Do Your Homework
There has been little written specifically on student-led cell groups, but a great deal has been written on adult cells and the cell church movement world-wide. The strategy and structure for adult cells will be your best starting point. Adapt what you can from adult materials to make it work — but don't let a lack of youth material stop you — the New Testament church didn't have materials and they did miraculous things through faith-based determination and being led by the Spirit.

### Develop Your Strategy
- How will you select and train your leaders?
- How will you disciple your leaders, and new converts?
- How will you track the success of your cell groups?

If you do not have a well thought out system, your ministry will unravel due to the rapid growth of youth cells.

### Communicate
People tend to be *down* on what they are not *up* on. A youth minister in Florida recently said, "We didn't want to rush things and end up shooting ourselves in the foot. We knew when we started we wanted to have the best start possible. Months ago, we shared the concept of cell ministry with our commission for youth and families. They got excited about it and voted to support it in whatever way necessary. From there, I took the plan

to the youth leadership board who also got excited and couldn't wait to begin.

"From there we talked the ministry up to individuals, adults, youth, and just about anyone who would listen. Once we had enough general excitement we held an introductory meeting open to all youth and adults." This youth pastor went on to talk about his strategy to accomplish his transition.

### Model Cell Life
For most of us, a shift from programs to relationship building will be a jolt. At the same time, it can set you free. A youth pastor at a recent conference reported, "I learned more in an hour and a half of a model cell group with my youth than I did in a year and a half of ministering to them with my program format."

### Draw in Your Potential Leaders
Model cell life for both students and adults alike. Help them develop their gifts and talents and minister to their needs.

### Mobilize
Train and equip your student and adult leadership. Develop a strong prayer base, model cell life and let your first leaders lead in a training environment. Help them succeed as leaders. Do an all day training event to bring everybody up to speed on where you are going and how you will get there.

### Launch
Go for it! Realize that failure comes with the territory. You will learn more by failure than by success. If you have truly been called, He will help you through the transition and equip you along the way. Begin your first cells.

### Ongoing Training
You can only grow as large as the leaders you produce. Pour your life into potential leaders and current leaders.

Students today face incredible challenges. Are you structured to impact their life? You cannot do it alone — train and equip the students. God gave you the love of Christ and the Gospel to take to this generation of "walking wounded." Make a strategy today!

# 27

## Youths Mentoring Youths
### The Life Blood of Youth Cell Ministry
by Marvin Jacobo

*Marvin Jacobo is Associate Minister of High School Ministries at First Baptist Church of Modesto, California, and ministers to 372 high schoolers weekly in small groups. First Baptist also has 225 junior highers and 125 young adults (college age) weekly in small groups. Marvin and his wife, Cheryl, have two daughters, Dayna and Danyel.*

Brett Butler, the all-star center fielder for the Los Angeles Dodgers, thought he needed a tonsillectomy. He discovered he had throat cancer. He was forced to quit baseball for the rest of the season and, eventually, his career. Though the LA Dodgers lost a star player, they didn't need to trade. Months before Butler discovered he had cancer, he took Roger Cedeno and mentored him. During spring training, Butler was at Dodgertown at 8:30 every morning coaching Cedeno. When Cedeno had his break, he did not forget who trained and prepared him for the task. *USA Today* quoted Cedeno in their May 1996 issue saying, "Maybe someday, if I have been around that long. I can help a young player like he helped me."

Much like Butler's dedication, it is the dedication of youths mentoring other youths that is the life blood of youth cells. We are only as good as our transfer of leadership from one person to the next. Youths must seek the best way to raise up future leaders. What steps can you, as a youth leader, take to bring an individual from participating in a cell to leading one?

### Spot (Matthew 4:18)

The first step in this transfer of leadership is to pray and identify those peers and youths who are likely candidates. You must look for those into whom you can pour your life — a "Cedeno."

You can spot a "called" one by their ability to connect seemingly unrelated ideas to life with Biblical truths and revelations. These individuals are excited about cells and able to see the "big picture."

They attempt to understand the goals in the cell and are curious about why the youth leader does what he does. These individuals encourage the leader and contribute positively in the cell instead of distracting or disrupting. They are usually creative, helpful and passionate. They want to take risks and are not afraid of failure. In fact, they see mistakes as opportunities for growth. They are available and make time for the leader and for discipling.

Once you identify such a person, the next step is to coach them. Develop a relationship with a disciple-making direction.

### Invite (Matthew 4:18)

Invite your prospect to come and work with you. Give them a vision of what they can become for Christ and His Kingdom. "Follow me, and I will show you how to lead a cell."

### Be Transparent (Matthew 26:36-46)

Your disciple will only be as honest about his life as you are about yours. If you share with him, he will feel free to share his life with you and deal with real issues. Model a healthy and Godly living in school, family and relationships with friends.

### Build Up (John 14:12)

Work with the unique strengths of your disciple to help him succeed. Do not force your disciple to be like you; rather, make him to be like Jesus Christ. Do not allow insecurities or pride to keep you from allowing your disciple to do greater things. Force them to stretch their limits!

### Restore

In love, show your disciple where he needs attention in his own life. Galatians 6:1 says to gently restore him with humility. Remember that there but by the grace God go you. Use the scriptures to help him see his faults and weaknesses (2 Tim 3:16-17) and help him learn from them. Don't "rescue" them; allow them to fail — and grow!

## Communicate (Mark 3:13)

More is caught than taught in the learning process. What you need to develop is a relationship. This takes commitment on your end to spend time with your disciple and explain why you do what you do in your cell. Share your heart with him. Allow him to see the vision God has given you. Communicate your passions. Jesus called his disciples to "be with Him," so take your potential leader with you as much as possible.

## Accept (John 21:15-23)

Jesus accepted Peter even after Peter denied Him three times. Give that same love and concern for your disciple as well as the freedom to fall. He will learn more from mistakes than from victories.

## Be Patient (Luke 22:31)

It takes time for people to change. Your disciple will not grow according to your timetable. Allow God the time to do his work in changing your disciple. Care about him as a person and not a project. Discover where the Holy Spirit is working in his life and focus your attention there. You will be more successful with him when you allow God to change him rather than forcing him into your preconceived ideas of success.

## Protect

Protect your disciple from dumb choices that will hurt him. Protect him also from others who will try to discourage him. Others will attack him for making mistakes, and he will need you to defend and support him through these difficult times. Give him the benefit of the doubt, that his motives were pure. Don't "save" him, but allow him to "handle" the situation with your support.

## Send

After you have done your role to disciple, seek God about His timing to release him. At some point you need to trust God and let them go. If you see consistent growth in your disciple's spiritual appetite — in reflecting the fruit of the Holy Spirit and in personal integrity — it may be time to release him. Your disciple may think he is not ready, but you need to encourage him. Brett Butler was effective through his humble investments in the lives of others. In this same way, the only way for youths to effectively pass on the mantle of leadership to another is by investing in the lives in their disciple. Develop these relationships, and have fun!

# Mobilizing Leaders
## Through Equipping

# Section 8

# 28

## The Ministry Education that Never Stops
### The Cell Church's Answer to Traditional
### Program-based Education
by Ralph W. Neighbour, Jr.

There is a very interesting fact buried in the book of Acts: no man, including Paul, ever went out to plant a church until he had first experienced a church being planted. Barnabas saw the Jerusalem plant before going to help in the Antioch plant. Saul of Tarsus spent up to four years in Antioch before being set apart as an apostle to Asia. Timothy experienced the planting in his hometown before Paul seconded him to go on the road with him. In Act 20, Paul's team included Sopater from Berea, Aristarchus and Secundus from Thessalonica, Galus from Derbe, Timothy also, and Tychicus and Trophimus from the province of Asia. In every case, these men had participated in church plants before they began to go to new places to establish Basic Christian Communities.

Some years ago, a large southern denomination hired me as a church planting consultant to help some young seminary graduates appointed to start new work in Chicago, Detroit, and Pittsburgh. I flew to these places on a regular basis to work with the fine young couples who were trying to do something they had never, ever experienced. All they had was a PBD church in their past and years in a seminary classroom. Out of the five couples, exactly five failed in their assignments. Three of the five quit the ministry, deeply discouraged.

During that time, I began to realize the PBD church had a huge problem. The way they designed their schools for Christian workers caused great frustration. Later, while on the faculty of a seminary, the President showed me a letter sent out by the heads of independent missionary societies to a number of Bible schools, colleges, and seminaries. It explained that they had been surveying the effectiveness of their overseas workers. They discovered that the least productive of the group were those with seminary degrees. The most effective were those who had a couple of years at the most in a Bible school! They were asking the seminary Presidents, "What are you doing to your students?"

As a faculty member of a seminary and a guest lecturer in over a dozen more, I knew the answer immediately. Take a young couple with fire in their bones and stick them in the artificial atmosphere of a seminary or a Bible school for three or four years. Next, send them to a strange land where they can't talk to anyone for another three or four years while they learn a new language — and what do you have? A burned out cinder of a live coal.

I shall never forget a visit to one missionary in Frankfurt who, after eleven years of "ministry," had eleven people in his living room on Sunday morning of his "worship service." On the third level of his home, he had built by hand a huge office with books lining each wall. He had hibernated there while drawing over $55,000 a year from the USA to be a "church planter." He didn't have a clue about what to do. He was "meeting his neighbors" in an attempt to "reach out." No urban strategy. No long range goals. Worst of all, no self-starting blood in his veins.

Many dear Christian workers in America suffer from this same disease. An institutional training for ministry is often the kiss of death. In one seminary faculty meeting, I suggested that our task was to prepare men and women to apply their trade, similar to a trade school for beauticians, mechanics or meat cutters. Whew! That didn't sit well at all!

But truth cannot be denied. Three years of revolving between the dorm, the classroom, the library, and the dining hall provides nothing but cognitive input that is often irrelevant when planting a church.

I recently visited a 90,000 member cell church in El Salvador. When I asked one of the zone pastors to show me their written materials for equipping all these people, he gave me a blank stare. I finally received one sheet of paper, printed on one side, which was given to their cell leader interns! In that semi-literate society, they had learned that the only way to equip people was "show and tell." It worked like a charm! Taking new believers by the hand, each cell member demonstrated how to visit the lost, how to arrange a room for a cell meeting, how to pray for the sick.

In other words, they were doing it like they did in the book of Acts. Every new cell member experienced a cell being established before being invited to be a cell leader intern. They not only experienced astonishing growth but also gave a living illustration of what has to happen in the cell churches of this generation.

With this philosophy in our hearts, Faith Community Baptist Church in Singapore has developed equipping tracks for all of our cell members, extending from conversion all the way to a ten-month course to prepare zone pastors for their ministries. Now in its third year, we are still learning lessons every day to help us tomorrow. We are ready to share our findings, with the caution that it takes more years than we have yet invested to get the "bugs" worked out.

Here are the stages we are currently using:

### 1. The Year of Equipping Track

When a new member enters a cell, a visit is made by the cell leader and a "sponsor" who has been selected to guide this person on the journey. During that "year" (which may take longer than twelve months) the new cell member is lovingly guided through a journey into his or her values, a survey of the Bible from cover to cover, and is taught how to reach out to both the easy-to-reach and hard-to-reach unbelievers.

### 2. Cell Leader's Equipping Track

There follows a six month internship as a cell leader and another six months of experience as a cell leader. This is under the supervision of an experienced cell leader. *The Shepherd's Guidebook* and the *Cell Leader's Guidebook* are written to steer this part of the journey.

### 3. Zone Supervisor's Equipping Track

Using the *Zone Supervisor's Guidebook*, the intern is apprenticed to a veteran Zone Supervisor for six months of training and another six months of supervised experience. The pastoral team selects those who are gifted and prepared for the next level of leadership.

### 4. Zone Pastor's Equipping Track

With a small salary to supplement this portion of the training, the zone pastor intern comes on staff and attends a ten-month zone pastor's training, nicknamed "TESS." Four mornings a week, the Intern attends classes which prepare him or her specifically for the ministry level of a zone pastor. In addition to the courses relating to the skills of guiding a zone of cell groups, the zone pastor intern will receive training in Bible study, doctrine, and counseling skills. All these courses are currently being created on videotape with student workbooks. Classes consist of a twenty to thirty minute video session, followed by twenty to thirty minutes of small group interaction by the class members in groups of five or six. Thus, the actual method of equipping is compatible with the relational lifestyle of the cell church.

The balance of the intern's week is spent working under the supervision of a zone pastor in the zone itself. Thus, the main portion of the equipping is at the level of apprenticeship — "on-the-job" training.

We have been quite satisfied with those taking this training. We are also sending out our own missionaries from our cell groups. Those who complete "TESS' and are assigned to a church planting team take additional modules related to cross-cultural subjects. This requires another full year of classes and ministry experience with the team in a cross-cultural setting.

By the end of 1994, "TESS" will be established first in the United States at the Cornerstone Church in Broadway, Virginia. Student enrollment will be limited to the number of outside students the church feels it can assimilate. Only full blown cell churches are eligible for setting up "TESS" zone pastor's training. This is crucial, since the most important part of the training is on-th-job, not is the classroom.

### 5. Senior Pastor's Equipping Track

We have already celebrated the presence of men on our staff who are created by God for ministry at the senior pastor's level. At our own expense, we are now beginning to send zone/district pastors to a formal seminary for training in Greek, Hebrew, Biblical exegesis, etc. The place of the traditional seminary with its scholars will be greatly needed and used in the years to come for sharpening the skills of preachers and teachers. Hopefully, some innovative traditional seminary in this world will realize the unlimited potential for "plugging in" to the direction of the cell church, and offer special "tracks" for those who have no interest in the paper chase, but simply want to soak up Biblical studies for use in their pulpits.

# 29

## Freedom:
### We All Want It, But are We Willing to Pay the Price to get it?
by Jim Egli

A young lady sitting near the front shook with frenzy while I was teaching. Her body went rigid, and the manifestations were clearly demonic. I was a young missionary halfway across the world ministering among the Xhosa people in Umtata, South Africa. I did not know what to do and neither did the African Christians present at the session. Satan wanted to disrupt the training, and he succeeded! This was my first face-to-face encounter with the demonic.

Four years later, instead of being a young, inexperienced missionary, I was a young, inexperienced pastor serving a small, rural church in central Illinois. Late one evening, my wife and I were counseling a young farm couple across our kitchen table. Their marriage was struggling, and the small fortune they had spent on professional counseling had done little good. When we stopped to pray with them, the wife said, "I see something evil. There is a dark presence that I can see in my mind trying to crush me." Again, I did not know what to do, but a novel thought occurred to me, "Pray!" As we sought God, the Holy Spirit brought step-by-step direction. There was victory, and the young wife then experienced the presence of God's Spirit in a new and wonderful way.

These two situations revealed to me that demons are just as real in little country churches in America as they are in Africa. In Africa they work overtly. In North America, they operate covertly. But their intent is the same: to destroy lives, marriages, churches and my teaching sessions. My experience also showed me that God wants to gloriously set people free and empower them with His Spirit!

## The Journey to Freedom

Without freedom, cell members fail to walk in the life God has for them. They will come to cell meetings, but they may have a neutral or even negative effect on the ministry of the group.

Without freedom, cell leaders may ask all of the right questions and fill out all the correct forms, but they will seldom see the power of God flow through them to minister to others. Without freedom, cell groups will not reach the lost because they will be preoccupied with their own problems.

Early in my ministry I realized that I needed to learn how to lead others into freedom. To learn how to do this, my wife and I attended four intensive one-week training sessions taught by Anne White of Victorious Ministry Through Christ. When I got to the first seminar, I discovered that the first step in learning to minister spiritual freedom to others began with me. In about four hours, several prayer ministers led me through a long, hard look at my past and bring every area of my life and history into submission under Christ. In this loving atmosphere, I brought to God areas from my past that I had never examined before. As I shared about key relationships, I confessed sin and released resentments.

Even though this did not feel like a mountaintop experience for me, I noticed profound changes in my life. First, I experienced a freedom in my thought life that I did not know was possible. For men, sexual thoughts are often a constant temptation. After my personal prayer ministry, sexual thoughts might have been tempting, but they were no longer controlling. Why? Because lurid images from films and magazines that I had experienced had now been specifically brought to the Lord. These images were removed from my mind and subconscious, and their power had been broken.

I also saw significant changes in my memories of childhood. I grew up in a solid Christian home, but like everyone, my childhood years were not perfect. Before this healing experience, when I recalled my childhood I would often remember hurt and disappointment. If I tried hard I could also remember many good things. After receiving ministry, it was just the opposite. The good things came to mind first. It now took effort to remember the bad things.

I had gone to the first training event to learn how to minister spiritual freedom. But I came away with more than know-how; I was now free to serve! There was a new level of victory in my life, a fresh sensitivity to the Spirit and a growing use of spiritual gifts in my ministry to others.

As you consider this subject, ask yourself: "Do I want a deeper experience of Christ's freedom and joy in my life?" And, "Do I want to learn how to minister healing and freedom to others in a deeper way?" If your answer to either of these questions is "yes," read on.

## Do You Want to Be Healed?

"Why do I have to confess my sins to you? Can't I just confess them to God?" Ted asked this question in a ministry session as he told us about an ugly part of his life. He asked a good question, and it might be one you have yourself. Can you confess your sins directly to God? Of course, you can! And when you do, God promises you total cleansing and forgiveness! His word assures us that, "If we confess our sins, he is faithful and just and will forgive us our sins and purify us from all unrighteousness" (1 John 1:9). But we are not talking about forgiveness. We are concerned with the issue of healing. The same Bible that guarantees forgiveness when we confess our sins to God, also tells us *"confess your sins to each other and pray for each other so that you may be healed"* (James 5:16, emphasis mine). If you need forgiveness, the Bible instructs you to confess your sins to God. If you need a deeper healing, it encourages you to seek ministry from others.

## It All Begins with You!

Do you need a deeper work of healing in your own life right now? Do you want to learn to minister spiritual victory to others? Either way, this ministry must begin with your own spiritual freedom. If you are a cell member or cell leader, talk to your pastor to see what freedom ministry your church offers. If your church does not have people trained in this ministry, ask your pastor where you might look for help. This type of ministry makes you realize the importance of submission to those over you in the Lord. (See 1 Thessalonians 5:12-13.) Satan loves to get believers unconnected and unprotected. Don't even think about beginning any type of spiritual freedom ministry without the blessing and counsel of your pastor!

There is likely someone trained in freedom ministry in your church or area who can help you. If not, learn about it by reading Neil Anderson's *The Bondage Breaker* and his practical ministry booklet *The Steps to Freedom in Christ*. Both are published by Gospel Light. Two other excellent books are the practical *The Believer's Guide to Spiritual Warfare* by Thomas B. White (Vine Books) and the explanatory *Spiritual Warfare* by Timothy Warner (Crossway Books).

## How to Minister Spiritual Victory to Others

If you are just beginning to minister to people in the area of spiritual victory and healing, I want to offer you some advice.

In John 5:6, Jesus asked a paralytic man, "Do you want to be healed?" Take note of his response. Instead of answering Jesus' question, he immediately made excuses. Often, people beginning a freedom ministry mistakenly attempt to help people who are not seeking healing and freedom. You may think that everyone wants to be healed. But it is easy for any of us to get comfortable with "my" problems and to actually depend on them.

When someone asks my wife or me to pray with them and minister to them in the areas of spiritual freedom and healing, we ask them some direct questions: "Do you really want to be set free? Are you ready to forgive others? Are you willing to quit blaming others and take responsibility for your future with God's help? Are you actively involved in a cell group? Are you in submission to those in authority over you?" If the answer is "no" to any of these questions, tell him or her to come back to you when the answers are "yes." Attempting to help people who are not ready is a waste of everyone's time. Dion Robert, the pastor of one of the world's largest churches in the Ivory Coast, Africa was asked at a conference what to do with cell members who don't want to deal with their personal bondages. Pastor Dion responded, "Nothing." He explained that it is better
to wait until people are miserable and genuinely want help.

Jesus told the paralytic man, "Pick up your mat and walk." (John 5:8) It is interesting that Jesus did not reach out and touch the man. Instead, he commanded him to do something that required personal initiative. If someone wants freedom ministry ask them to take the first step. People that want freedom counseling in the cell ministry at our church are required to have read *The New Believer's Station*. We require this book because it makes people interactively study what the Bible says about strongholds, forgiving others and the lordship of Christ. Now that our church is offering Encounter weekends, they are also prerequisites to individual sessions. These weekends convey essential teaching on spiritual warfare and they deepen the body life relationships that help believers — especially new Christians — walk out their victory.

## Going Deep in Personal Ministry

What takes place in a prayer ministry session that is focused on spiritual freedom? It is not that complicated. Your simple goal is to help individuals bring everything to God that is holding them back from total surrender to Jesus Christ. To do this, address three areas. First, guide people to confess their sin to God. Second, walk them through forgiving those that have hurt them. Thirdly, break the power of spiritual oppression that has come to them through their sins, through hurts or through lies or curses that have been spoken over them. Sessions do not have to be dramatic and emotional. Demonic oppression is usually easy to deal with once you have dealt with the underlying roots. Different books and ministries commend various patterns, but they all boil down to these three elements of inviting the Holy Spirit to do His revealing work. He desires to bring deep healing, and He will if you wait on Him and listen to His directions. As you listen to people confess, also listen to the Holy Spirit. As you pray for them, be sensitive to His timing and guidance. I remember one session when I was ministering to a middle-aged man. As we prayed for him, in my mind I saw a young boy getting out of a car. When I shared this with him, he immediately knew what it meant. His son had missed the school bus the day before, and the man had to drive him to school. He was very upset which caused him to belittle the child. This was not an isolated incident; it was an ongoing pattern in a deteriorating relationship. Through this word of knowledge, God revealed his need to repent of his attitudes as a father.

One of the most rewarding things in this ministry is seeing the Holy Spirit's gentle, probing work as people come to God for healing. He can move through you this way also. You don't have to sit as you listen to a cell member complain about the same sin for the forty-second time. You can learn to lead people into freedom. And you can be free yourself to love people as never before!

# 30

## Sponsoring Inspires Godly Growth
### Genuine Love and Encouragement Help Others Mature
by Vicki Egli

*Vicki Egli and her husband Jim oversee the small group ministry of the Vineyard Church in Champaign-Urbana, Illinois. She is a writer and trainer who especially enjoys discipling new Christians and women leaders. She and Jim have three young adult sons and a nine-year-old daughter.*

*"But encourage one another daily, as long as it is called Today, so that none of you may be hardened by sin's deceitfulness."* — Heb. 3:13

In life's busyness, it's easy to miss our daily dose of spiritual encouragement. Sponsoring a "younger" Christian, someone who is spiritually less mature than yourself, is one of the best ways to keep both yourself and your sponsee growing in Christ.

### Why Should I Sponsor?

Much of Jesus' ministry was devoted to teaching his twelve disciples. A significant portion of that time was spent with only Peter, James and John. Jesus invested Himself in those three and reaped tremendous results years later as they led the early church. As you invest in others, they will be more fruitful in the Kingdom.

Perhaps the benefits of sponsoring are obvious to you. Sponsoring increases your dependency on the Holy Spirit and strengthens your faith as you view Him at work in another. It gives you the opportunity to strengthen your weaker areas, which are exposed as you share frankly with your sponsee. The sponsoring process reproduces your life in Christ in someone else. You will see that person grow into maturity and lead others into a deeper walk with Christ.

### Whom to Sponsor?

Most new Christians long for someone to offer friendship and support to them. For that matter, don't we all? Let your cell leader or pastor know that you feel called to sponsor someone, and then they can pray with you for discernment. If you don't know a new Christian, they probably do and can help you find the right person. You may be older or younger than your sponsee, richer or poorer, more or less educated. But to protect yourselves in these intimate relationships, the sponsor and sponsee must be of the same gender.

## What Do Sponsors Do?

Love is the core of sponsoring. You have received God's unconditional love and so are able to extend that love to your sponsee. You will pray daily for her, weep and laugh with her, challenge her. But you will not, and must not try to, solve all her problems or answer all her questions.

You will reflect on the basics of the Christian life together, discussing such things as freedom from sin, baptism, daily time with the Lord, the Holy Spirit and evangelism. You will help connect her with the larger body of Christ and encourage her to take advantage of all the church has to offer. You will model the Christian life and prepare her to sponsor a new believer.

You also will meet with your sponsee each week, and this is one of the blessings of sponsoring. Be flexible about when and where to meet. Find a place and time that works into both of your schedules, whether it's early in the morning, over lunch, or after kids are in bed. This is your time together, away from interruptions. Make time for it every week.

When you meet, pray for the Holy Spirit's guidance and then bring each other up-to-date on what's happening in your lives. Dig into any equipping materials you may be journeying through, and share Bible memory verses. Actively listen to your sponsee while also listening to what the Holy Spirit is speaking to you. Prayerfully wrestle with the issues your sponsee is facing. Share of God's goodness and extend His grace to your sponsee. As she shares from her life and you interact with the equipping materials, the Holy Spirit will uncover issues that need to be addressed and give you words to encourage, comfort, challenge or teach. End your time with prayer, and plan for the coming weeks. As the sponsor, you are responsible for preparing for the next meeting, faithfully following directions given through your church or the material you're using.

Being in touch with each other throughout the week strengthens the sponsoring relationship. How much time you spend with your sponsee apart from the weekly meeting will vary greatly, depending on how the Lord wants to use you. Will you play the part of an older sister? You may go shopping or clean house together. Does He want you to walk with your sponsee through a spouse's painful breech of trust? You may talk on the phone for a half-hour each day, and meet for lunch once a week. As partners in evangelism, you may work out together at the gym or meet at the park with other moms of young children. Whatever the dynamics of the relationship, the Lord will be able to use you more effectively in your sponsee's life as you make time in your weekly schedule for her.

## When Crisis Arises

In times of crisis, give of yourself to your sponsee. Pray for discernment about your role. Pray diligently. Most often, the Lord also wants to include others to minister to your sponsee, so avoid trying to meet every need that arises. Does your sponsee need a pastor, a mechanic, a financial consultant? Lovingly connect your sponsee to those who can most effectively minister in the situation.

One sponsee, Cheri, had been a believer for some time, but she was discontent with her lifestyle. She was ready to deal with and overcome certain habits and attitudes in her life. Sensing her spiritual openness, I asked my cell leader if I could sponsor her. We shared our spiritual pilgrimages the first two times we met, and then we started studying The New Believer's Station. We talked and prayed about listening to the Lord, receiving and living out Christ's freedom, following Jesus as Lord, and growing in God's Word. I delighted in seeing the Lord work in a life open to Him! God's Word transformed Cheri right before my eyes. She shared what God was saying to her, and we felt God's presence with us and pleasure in us. We tasted His goodness, and I smelled the sweet aroma of Christ in Cheri.

Everything seemed to be moving along so smoothly. Then Cheri's world came crashing in when she discovered that her husband had hidden an undelt-with sin from her for years. Her response to the situation was to question the wisdom of keeping their family intact. She found out on Wednesday. Our accountability time was Thursday. Thank God she had the courage to share her struggle with me. We cried and prayed together. Her desire was for her husband to confess his sin to the cell leader and ask for help, so she asked me to keep the information confidential. I sensed that God wanted me to keep the confidence and watch Him work, so this was a time of fasting and prayer for me. The sin was exposed, and her husband sought counseling.

Cheri had many Christian friends to support her and speak Scripture into her life. Satan tried to confuse the situation, but Cheri stood firm and obeyed God because she was confident that she had discerned His voice. She knew I (and other cell members and Christian friends) would challenge her to be faithful to her calling in Christ Jesus.

"Instead, speaking the truth in love, we will in all things grow up into him who is the Head, that is, Christ. From him the whole body, joined and held together by every supporting ligament, grows and builds itself up in love, as each part does its work" (Ephesians 4:15-16).

Don't try to be the whole body. Be faithful to do your part and allow others to do theirs, and your sponsee will be built up into Christ.

# 31

## Feasting on Between-Meal Snacks
### 'Family' Relational Time Whets Appetites
### for More Togetherness
by Randall G. Neighbour

I have spent hundreds of hours in cell meetings experiencing incredible times of worship, learning, and giving and receiving ministry. These weekly meetings were exciting and balanced when cell members immersed themselves in ministry, discipleship and lifestyle evangelism during the week. But when members didn't have a clue about living in Christian community, the meeting time felt rushed and insufficient to meet the group's needs, or we were just plain bored because no one felt comfortable enough to enter into worship and ministry.

Conversely, the hours invested in discipling cell members, helping them move furniture and coaxing them into joining me in building projects outnumber the meeting times tenfold. Meetings fade away, but memories of kingdom-building activities are precious and remain forever.

### Help-full Kingdom-Building

I'll never forget kingdom-building with my friend Harry. He was a single guy about my age who bought an old house in the same neighborhood as my wife and me. Our common bonds were (1) Jesus and (2) the urge to use power tools on the other guy's house, in that order.

Harry was my cell leader; I was his intern. We prayed together for hours each week, lifting our cell members and the lost to the Lord. We ministered to a Chinese couple by helping them with transportation to and from cell meetings and Sunday celebrations.

With the prayers and assistance of the rest of the cell, they became followers of Jesus.

Did our stellar cell meetings make us successful kingdom-builders? Not so you could notice! We messed up most of the cell agendas and stumbled through ministry time week after week. Without Harry's determination week in and week out to move every cell member into a lifestyle of helping others and to model this for me, we would have dissolved the cell and joined a garden club.

Harry knew that the best way to build community was to ask for help and to offer it as often as possible, so he focused on between-meeting ministry opportunities. As I reflect on that, I see that our prayer time prepared our hearts and gave us a hunger for servanthood. We gave the daily interaction among cell members as much clout as those weekly meetings, and our cell grew and increased the kingdom of God.

## Snacks and Dinner Too!

Between-meal snacks were frowned upon in my mother's kitchen. If I filled up on potato chips or cookies after school, my mother was certain my appetite would be spoiled and I wouldn't eat all those nutritious vegetables served at dinner. Truthfully, I could inhale every scrap of food in the house at 4 p.m. and still eat seconds at the dinner table. I was a growing boy and a voracious eating machine.

Dinner at our home was a spectacular daily event. My two older brothers and I would sit at the table and impatiently wait for the blessing. Dad often would give thanks (my mother liked to pray for all the missionaries before she asked God to bless the food) and then we'd dig in. My mom prepared the best food in the whole world. I don't remember all the dishes she cooked, but I clearly recall the times we laughed and talked and loved each other's company as a family should. I often invited my friends to stay for dinner, and many of them came to know my parents as Uncle Ralph and Aunt Ruth. Our meal times weren't an exclusive event, but my parents understood that daily interaction among the family members would keep us strong and prevent us from growing apart.

## Family Community

Your family of origin may not have looked like mine. But your cell "family" should resemble the dinner table of a healthy family:

- Get together with members outside your weekly meeting time to fellowship, share dreams and discuss problems. Make these "between-meeting snacks" a priority. They will increase your appetite and whet it for more relational time, not spoil it!
- Pray together whenever possible. This keeps the group's focus on Jesus and on the need to share Him with others.
- Look for ways to meet each other's needs. If your members aren't comfortable enough yet to let you serve them, ask them to do something for you.
- Invite outsiders to partake of "between-meeting snacks" before you invite them to a cell meeting. They will see how real you are and how real Jesus is inside you.

A few months ago, Harry and I took our wives to get an ice cream cone and catch up. He's a married man of a few years now and lives in the suburbs. We don't even go to the same church any more, so visits like these are special. While we talked about those days of close friendship and teamwork, we recognized that God had placed us together for a season to learn, grow and model that selfless lifestyle for others.

The ironic thing about cell-based community is that God gives it to us to achieve something very special for a short period of time. We shouldn't look at community as a goal. It's a gift God gives us because it's one of the most powerful tools we have to minister to each other and reach our world for Jesus.

# 32

## A Time To Be Fathers
### Mentoring in the Cell Church
by Billy Hornsby

*Billy Hornsby is the director of Bethany Cell Church Network in Baker, Louisana.*

The greatest desire in the heart of a young son or daughter is to have a strong loving relationship with his or her father. Depending on the statistics you read, the typical father in America spends an average of thirty seconds to seven minutes per day in meaningful conversation with his children. The increasing number of single parent families in our world reflects a parallel concern in the House of Faith. We are out of practice in training our spiritual offspring! As leaders, we must refocus and reprioritize our time for the sake of those who look up to us for discipleship and spiritual fatherhood. They need mentors. An overwhelming percentage of Christians — especially new converts—are raised up in the Church without a Christian father figure to guide them in their journey. Across the social lines of boomers, busters, and Gen X, there is many a "Timothy" looking for a "Paul." Without a strong mentor, millions of Christians will never reach spiritual maturity.

Relationships between spiritual leaders and most of the men and women in churches today are casual and non-committal. Typically, we make eye contact on Sunday morning and say, "How are you doing? Let's do lunch sometime." This false attempt at friendship never satisfies the yearning in the hearts of those who need a mentor. God's plan for "fathering" is clearly demonstrated in Romans, yet it is not always understood as a methodology. It must be employed by the Church if we desire to walk out our calling to disciple the nations.

A mentor wears many hats as a "father figure" in the church. He communicates values and passes down critical specialized information. He stands by as a counselor and advisor to help bring clarity to someone's life along the way. He passes on qualities to his disciple that are like spiritual vitamins and minerals, catalysts for digesting and assimilating spiritual truth and godly wisdom.

Seven titles describe the role that a mentor plays in the life of his disciple.

### 1. Discipler

He communicates the basics of following Christ. The discipler takes the disciple through the daily disciplines that help make them a successful and true follower of Christ. How to pray, build strong relationships, offer and receive forgiveness, walk in the Spirit and other important steps are taught in this caring relationship.

### 2. Spiritual Guide

He provides accountability and insight for maturity. To guide someone in spiritual matters is to help them understand the spiritual implications of events in everyday life. The disciple must learn to be accountable to someone who has walked the path before him and can bring correction and instruction with mature and productive methods.

### 3. Coach

He gives motivation and teaching skills for action. A coach shows his team members how to play the game with a victorious outcome. He knows the players and the skills in which they must improve to be their best. He provides encouragement and recognition while bringing them through the regiments of the game of life.

### 4. Counselor

He resolves problems in times of crisis and provides a mature perspective in a loving manner. One of the main roles of a counselor is to offer sound biblical advice on how Christians should relate to each other. This includes, but is not limited to spouses, children, co-workers, creditors and other Christians. The mentor in the role of the counselor must be sensitive to the disposition and maturity level of his disciple. A good mentor must convict and admonish yet endeavor to do so without alienating his disciple.

### 5. Teacher

He transfers knowledge and understanding of the issue at hand. The teacher is one who has learned the lessons in academics and through life experience and has the skill to pass on that information to the disciple as a student.

### 6. Sponsor

He provides opportunities for the disciple to discover the next step in his growth and keeps him connected to others who are important in his walk (most people stop the growing process when the next step is unclear). The sponsor has been down the road before and knows what to do next as well as who should come along side to help. He provides direction as well as relationship for the disciple.

### 7. Role Model

He becomes a living example to be emulated in all phases of life. Ninety percent of what we learn comes from what has been demonstrated for us. As the disciple observes the life of the mentor through a consistent time investment, he learns what to do in a given situation and how to give a Christ-like response. The writer of Hebrews admonishes us to "follow" the faith of those who have rule over us. It is the mentor's duty to provide a model that can be followed by others to the glory of God.

While every person in our lives is important to us, not all are to be considered "fathers." I Corinthians 4:15 states, "For though you have ten thousand instructors in Christ, you do not have many fathers . . ." Oh, that God would make each of us a father of many nations! If not a nation, then a father of twelve, like Jesus was with his disciples.

As you read this, are there believers in your church or cell that need your gifts and talents as a mentor? Cast off the "let's do lunch" attitude and put on the garment of mentorship!

# 33

## Kingly Cave Talk
### Follow in David's Footsteps to Develop Heroes for God
by James Bell

*James Bell is pastor of Hosanna Church in Houston, TX, where he and his wife, Suzanne, have pastored for 10 years.*

Scattered across the pages of the biblical account of David's life are tales of unparalleled heroism by a group known as David's Mighty Men. These men killed giants, won spectacular victories and became legendary. But look at how they started. Members of David's first recruiting class were described as distressed, indebted and discontent. And their meeting place was in a cave!

*So David departed from there and escaped to the cave of Adullam; and when his brothers and all his father's household heard of it, they went down there to him. And everyone who was in distress, and everyone who was in debt, and everyone who was discontented, gathered to him; and he became captain over them. — 1 Samuel 22:1-2*

What happened to those guys? How did such hopeless people become heroes? What caused society's rejects to grow into an elite fighting force? It all began with cave talk. The process was one of changing core values and shifting, if not shattering, paradigms.

When these men came to David, he was at a low place in his life, too. The giddy thrill of victory swirled around him at an early age. He became a national hero. When he was just a boy, Israel's prophet-priest Samuel anointed him to be king. But from the palace of King Saul, he experienced a free-fall to the depths of rejection. Then he hid, fearing for his life. It appeared that his best days were over. This was not a good time to hold a seminar on self-esteem!

But they came anyway. Ragged, discouraged, desperate men

crowded into the cave. David must have looked over the group, brushed aside the memories of the disciplined troops he had known and fought with, and realized that his only hope was God.

This is certainly relevant when you look up from your cell material one night to realize that some of your sheep look more like creatures from the Black Lagoon. Not that they have a scary physical appearance, but because strongholds are towering above everything else in their lives. And now their eyes are upon you, their leader.

So what is a godly leader to do? One cell leader said, "I gotta multiply my group fast. And I want to pick who goes!" Believe me, there is a better way. We can pick up some clues from David. He had a lot of success with turning his mess into a miracle.

David wrote Psalm 57 while he hid out in the cave. I often wonder whether he was speaking of those renegades living with him in the cave when he wrote in verse 4:

*My soul is among lions;*
*I must lie among those who breathe forth fire,*
*even the sons of men, whose teeth are spears and arrows,*
*and their tongue a sharp sword.*

Now imagine that this verse was a description of your cell group. It would be pretty tough to whip those folks into shape, huh? Let's face it: Most of us would quickly realize that we were not capable of performing the task. Well, that is exactly what David concluded! In verse 2 of that same Psalm, he wrote,

*I will cry to God Most High,*
*to God who accomplishes all things for me.*

We have to understand that God is capable of accomplishing anything. Now think about that for a moment. After all, He saved you! God can do anything, and He is available to help you. That's a powerful thought. So we bring our group daily before the Lord. We ask for wisdom and guidance in leading them. We expect God to start accomplishing things! Another insight into how God does this kind of thing is found in the latter part of verse 3,

*God will send forth His lovingkindness and His truth.*

When you deal with challenging people entrusted your care, always make sure that your love-ometer is registering higher than your truth-ometer. And also be aware that you must have both of these divine weapons of spiritual warfare. The combination of love and truth is what triumphs when spiritual strongholds are approached. David's cave talk undoubtedly encompassed much love and truth. So don't hold back the love that God pours through you. The unlovable need it the most. And when you know that people are aware that you love them, do not hold back the truth, either. Confronting in love is always necessary for effective leadership. In the ranks of our spiritual enemy, tolerance has as many kills as judgement.

It is comforting to know that God will send forth His love and truth to us. These come through our relationship with Him. How do we use love and truth? Well, how does He use them with you? Ministering out of your own experience with God keeps the truth sharp and accurate and the love fresh and sincere. So love, share the truth, and let God do the accomplishing. You will begin to see those folks with rough edges turning into mighty warriors for God.

David had a special love for those rag-tag fellows who came to him in the cave. When he later was crowned king of Israel, he appointed them as the special honor guard of the king. He must have cherished the way they marched, keeping rank with heads held high. He loved to tell of their exploits and acts of courage. But the really special ingredient in the diet of discipline and skill that he fed these men was His faith in God.

Browse through Psalm 57 and Psalm 34 again, and think about how God inspires us to inspire others. Listen hard to what David is saying. It is cave talk. And it will help you develop some heroes for God.

# Relational Evangelism in the Cell

# Section 9

# 34

## "I Sat in the Pew Frustrated, Again!"
### My Journey into Joyful Evangelism
by Jay Firebaugh

As the pastor preached that morning, I felt guilty about my lack of effort at soul winning. Yet every time I gathered my courage and forced myself to witness, it produced little except to raise my blood pressure and *frustration.*

For most of my life, this experience has represented my feelings about evangelism. I grew up in a Bible-teaching church where we were chided to "witness," but I don't remember many people actually doing it. Then I went to a Christian college and later to seminary, where we were challenged about the plight of "lost people." Still, only a handful of bold students tried to evangelize. I forced myself to share the Gospel with complete strangers a few times, but that was the extent of my efforts.

I didn't know how to evangelize back then. And my 15 years as a pastor have shown me that many others don't know how to "witness" either. We talk about evangelism, and we proclaim the Gospel. We celebrate when people come to know Christ, but evangelism for most of the folks in my church is something we hope "the other guy" will do.

This troubled the elders and staff of my church, so we evaluated the situation a few years back. Ours is a good-sized church that has consistently grown each year. But our research revealed that our growth came from Christians leaving their churches and coming to our church, not from new converts. Frankly, it bothered us that a church our size did not know how to bring more people to Christ.

## Primary Purpose

In Matthew 16:18, Jesus said to Peter, *". . . Upon this rock I will build my church, and all the powers of hell will not conquer it"* (New Living Translation). Certainly, whatever the church is about, doing battle against the forces of hell is at its heart! Ted Haggard, pastor of New Life Church in Colorado Springs, CO, came to the conclusion that, "I did not have the privilege of just reading my Bible, praying nice prayers and pastoring a pleasant little church. I had to rescue a lot of people from impending eternal disaster". (*Primary Purpose*, pgs. 29-30). That led Haggard and his church to conclude that their primary purpose was to make it hard for people of their city to go to hell.

Evangelism must be more than something we honor by talking about it, or something for those people especially gifted with boldness or skill at relating the Gospel. It must lie at the heart of why we exist as a church. And it must be something in which *everyone* (whether you have the gift of evangelism or not) is involved. This means that I, as a pastor, must take the lead and evangelize as well.

## Learning How To Evangelize

Our church was full of people who cared that others were lost and going to hell, but we never learned how to evangelize effectively. We didn't know how to reach out as a team and help unbelievers enter into a relationship with Christ. We didn't know how to care for people over time, through loving relationships. This is one of the discoveries that propelled us to begin our transition to a cell-based church. Cells are the perfect place to mobilize *all* Christians to reach unbelievers.

While cell groups are the most natural environment to enter this journey of relational evangelism, nothing is automatic. We learned that groups must take intentional steps to reach out and grow.

The first step developed out of our need to be intentional in our relationships with unbelievers. So our cells created lists of people whom group members believed God wanted to reach through them: neighbors, co-workers, friends and relatives, people with whom they spend time and develop relationships. These people form the immediate circle of relationships that make up each cell member's *oikos* (Greek for household or sphere of influence). This is the cell's *oikos* list. Everyone in the cell needs to pray for one or two unbelievers to come to know Christ.

Secondly, we realized that the battle is spiritual! The most important thing we can do for lost people is pray for them. Praying for our *oikos* should be a regular part of a cell gathering. 2 Corinthians 4:4 says, "The god of this age has blinded the minds of unbelievers, so that they cannot see the light of the Gospel of the glory of Christ, who is the image of God." The only reason someone can't see a need for Christ is because he or she has been blinded by satan. Only a person with a distorted vision of the truth can refuse a Savior who loves them so much that He gave His life to redeem them.

The solution is to battle through prayer. Our groups pray specifically against the roadblocks that stand in the way of these unbelievers seeing their need for Jesus. Maybe they're stumbling over the spiritual hypocrisy of others. Perhaps it's their own insecurity, foolish pursuit of fun or life on their own terms. It could be selfishness, or any number of strongholds such as addiction, lust, unforgiveness or pride. As the Holy Spirit gives discernment, we call out against the demonic grip that Satan has over these people and ask Jesus to break it so that their eyes may be opened.

As a cell gets serious about praying on behalf of *oikos* members, the list will cease to be the person "you" are burdened for and become the people "we" are burdened for. At this point, each cell member is evangelizing.

## Get in Their Boat

While praying, cell members also must increase relationships with the people for whom they are seeking the heart of God. Luke 5:1-3 reveals a great example from Jesus' life. "One day as Jesus was standing by the Lake of Gennesaret, with the people crowding around him and listening to the word of God, He saw at the water's edge two boats, left there by the fishermen, who were washing their nets. He got into one of the boats, the one belonging to Simon Peter, and asked him to put out a little from shore. Then He sat down and taught the people from the boat."

Jesus was teaching, but Simon Peter, for whom Jesus had a burden, was off to the side not listening. In order to get Peter's attention, Jesus got into his boat. To reach people for Christ, get their attention by "getting in their boat": build relationships, become their friend, and increase your connection with them.

After we moved into our new home last May, our children would stand on the wood pile behind our house and peer at the neighbor's kids over the wooden fence that separates our back yards. As the kids all started playing together, my wife and I felt called to get into the boat of our neighbors, Tod and Sandy. We prayed for them to come to Christ and built a relationship with them. We invited them over for burgers and ice cream. We went camping with them, and our kids continued to play together. Tod and I built a gate in the fence so we could easily walk between our back yards.

Meanwhile, our cell included Tod and Sandy on our *oikos* list for prayer. Each week we prayed for Tod and Sandy, even though no one in the cell knew them. Our cell members encouraged us to continue working on the relationship. Week in and week out, we did just that.

## Cell Bridge Events

After spending the summer building the relationship and praying for Tod and Sandy, we invited them to a cell bridge event, our Labor Day picnic. A bridge event can be a game night, picnic, dinner outing, etc. The important things are to hold these regularly (many of our cells aim for once a month), and for all members to understand that their job is to interact with the guests and help them feel welcome.

Tod and Sandy agreed to come to the cell's picnic, though they wanted to drive their own car so they'd have an escape. They didn't need it! They had a wonderful time, and the cell members were excited to meet the couple for whom they'd been praying.

It is important to understand how our cell worked together as a team. My family was working to get into Tod and Sandy's boat, but everyone in our cell was praying for and had a burden for Tod and Sandy. Everyone took ownership in our joint effort to love Tod and Sandy to Christ. And not only Tod and Sandy, but also the other unbelievers who were being reached by other cell members.

Now we had a relationship with Tod and Sandy, and so did others in our cell. The members grew those relationships. The women invited Sandy to go shopping with them and sent her notes of encouragement. The men invited Tod to play golf. Tod and Sandy came to our regular cell events. Then they began to ask questions about spiritual things. One Saturday night in November, Tod asked whether his family could join us at church on Sunday. When they arrived, they were greeted by their friends from the cell who sat with them and talked with them every step of the way.

Tod and Sandy started attending our cell. A few months later, Sandy prayed to receive Christ as her Savior. Tod did the same with one of the members of our cell in the church lobby after worship. Our entire cell went out to lunch afterward to celebrate with them. This family was reached because everyone in a cell worked together to see them come to know Christ. It started with a heartfelt burden for people who are spiritually lost and included a specific plan of prayer, relationships and regular cell events. We *all* worked together to evangelize.

## Re-Learning Evangelism

We're still learning to approach evangelism this way as a church, but the number of stories similar to those of Tod and Sandy is growing. Evangelism finally is a joy instead of a frustration. And it isn't something we just talk about. We partner with others in our cell to do something about it. We target people and challenge each other to get into their boats because we believe God will use us to reach them. It doesn't happen automatically. It takes purposeful, Holy Spirit-driven intervention. I am learning and relearning this over and over.

For example, I came home late from work the other night and a neighbor was out working on his car. I was tired and wanted go inside, take my shoes off and rest. But I knew my cell was going to ask me whether I was getting into Bill's boat. So I went over and crawled under the hood of his car with him. Another time, my wife wanted to invite my daughter's entire soccer team and their parents over for a potluck dinner. I initially thought of the hassle it would be. Then my wife reminded me again of the need to build relationships with these people, most of whom are lost. It is something we have to remind ourselves of continually.

But it works! It's exciting to see people effectively evangelize when they formerly thought they could never reach others for Christ. They learn to work together as a team — praying specifically, challenging one another, having events, and working hard to incorporate these people. They discover what really impacts unbelievers in positive ways so that they are open to the Good News of Jesus. They finally realize that guilt is not the way God motivates us to reach their friends.

I've met very few unbelievers who know they are lost. What's more, they aren't looking for God. Few non-Christians have friends who really care about them in a selfless, loving way. When your cell works together, you literally have the opportunity to love people into openness to the Gospel and into a saving relationship with Jesus Christ.

There is nothing more fulfilling than experiencing the joy of reaching out together. Just ask Tod and Sandy!

# 35

## The Fields are White
### How Can Cell Churches Bring People to Christ and Enfold Them in His Family?
by Jim Egli

First-time observers of the cell church movement are often amazed at the growth rate of cell churches, but a closer look reveals something even more remarkable about their growth. Cell churches grow primarily through conversions. This stands in sharp contrast to growing program-based churches in North America that grow overwhelmingly through transfer growth.

How do cell churches do evangelism? Why do they succeed where traditional churches fail? How do they bring people to Christ and enfold them in his body?

As I have researched cell churches around the world, I have seen several factors at work in church after church. These factors are passion, training, teamwork, and special events. I want to explain each one of these and then draw some practical conclusions for those just beginning to implement cell church principles.

### Passion

Effective outreach doesn't begin with techniques. It begins when we ask God to give us His heart for the lost. God's compassion moved Him to sacrifice even to the point of the death of His Son. Outreach is costly. We want it to be costless and comfortable. That's impossible. It will cost us our lives as we sacrifice our time, our agendas and ourselves. This kind of sacrifice comes only when we let God plant his heart for the lost in our own hearts.

## Training

In a number of surveys, the American Institute for Church Growth asked over 14,000 people the question, "Who or what was responsible for your coming to Christ and the church?" More than four out of five of these people said that they were influenced to receive Christ by a friend or relative. Extensive research in this area points to one simple truth: most people are brought to Christ by ordinary people who loved them and made Jesus real to them. Cell churches maximize this simple principle by training each believer in caring, relational outreach.

Different churches use different materials and training settings. In the "equipping track" developed by Ralph Neighbour, within six months after coming to Christ, new believers are given confidence to share their faith through *The Touching Hearts Guidebook*. Typically this training occurs in a one-on-one relationship within the cell or through a weekend seminar. This illustrates an important factor: people should be equipped to share their faith as soon as possible after receiving Christ because this is when they have the broadest network of non-Christian friends.

New Christians make great evangelists. In fact, pre-Christians sometimes are really good at evangelism. I remember a young woman in one of our cells who came for several months before she made a commitment to Christ. However, she was so excited about the love that she found there that she was weekly bringing friends and relatives, even before she was a Christian herself.

In the past we waited to equip people in evangelism until they were more "mature." Unfortunately, when we wait a year or more, they have often lost contact with their unbelieving friends and the relational bridges needed for the gospel to travel across are gone.

Evangelism equipping materials must have a deliberate plan for equipping the body that trains believers in the basics of loving others to Christ: relational outreach, prayer for the lost, cooperating with the Holy Spirit, how to share their testimony and how to share the good news of Jesus. Whether you use Ralph Neighbour's materials or others, you must think through and strategize how this training takes place in the flow of cell church life.

## Teamwork

Jesus said, "One sows, another reaps" (John 4:37). The implication is, evangelism takes more than one of us; it takes teamwork.

I like the way Win Arn put this in his *Master's Plan for Making Disciples*. "A non-Christian friend can see Jesus in me, but not in a complete way. The more Christians I introduce him to, the more completely he can see Christ." I have seen this truth repeated in my own outreach, and its reality is seen in cell churches around the world. Effective evangelism takes teamwork, and the most effective evangelism team is the cell.

When we introduce non-Christians to cell members, they see Him reflected in Christians' lives and in the relationships that we have with each other. Broken relationships fill the world around us, and when they see caring relationships, it grabs their attention. The Apostle John puts it this way, "No one has ever seen God; but if we love each other, God lives in us and his love is made complete in us" (1 John 4:12). In other words, the way God is going to become real to others is through our practical love for one another.

Cells can work at team evangelism in lots of ways:

- Pray weekly for the lost. Support each other in personal outreach;
- Plan social events every month or two that they can invite unbelievers to;
- Focus special care and prayer on two or three especially receptive unbelievers;
- Include one another in personal activities and events with non-Christian friends.
- Start sub-groups out of the cell geared toward unbelievers, such as interest groups or investigative Bible studies.

This sense of teamwork in cells is consistent. It is a part of their weekly agenda as they pray for outreach and encourage each other. It is deliberate as the cells plan events and sub-groups for outreach. The events are often parties or outings with the purpose of building relationships with non-Christians and introducing them to cell members. Special groups are also formed to appeal to the felt needs of those around them. For example, it's November as I write this. My cell is now planning a Christmas party in December where we will invite non-Christian friends. My wife and I also recently completed a parenting class that we led in our neighborhood for young parents. Only one couple from the cell was in the group of six couples, but another couple from the cell baby-sat for the class and everyone else prayed for the group. It was exciting and fun and now we are following through on the relationships formed there.

## Harvest Events

Cell churches around the world have "harvest events." Although these may be called different things in different locations, the same principles are at work. Several times a year there are high quality events where believers can easily invite non-Christians. These may by drama events, special Christmas services, crusades, musicals, or healing services.

At the rural church in which I pastored, we used these same principles in annual Invite-A-Friend Sundays and candlelight Christmas Eve services. We would print invitations for these events and soak them in prayer. Our attendance would typically jump 70% for these events.

At Faith Community Baptist Church in Singapore, they have a big musical every year called "Come, Celebrate Christmas!" Last year it drew a total attendance of 40,000 and the church recorded thousands of decisions for Christ that were followed up by the cell groups.

The name and shape of harvest events vary from place to place. But the principles remain the same. They are exciting, appealing events, soaked in prayer, that believers can enthusiastically invite friends to knowing that they'll have a great time and hear a clear and compelling presentation of the gospel.

## Getting Serious About Outreach

If you are just now beginning your cell journey, where do you start? I've got three "D's" for you. Do it, design it, and discern it.

### Do it.

The starting point is you. Are you personally reaching out to the lost? Is relational outreach a high priority in your own weekly schedule? Pastors, staff members and cell leaders must live relational outreach if it is to take root throughout the church.

There are different tools for getting serious. Even if you don't have cells in place yet, start using an evangelism tool in existing classes or programs to put the values in place that will make the cells effective. Watch out, though, it may change your lives! Excellent resources include: *The Master's Plan* by Win Arn, *The Touching Hearts Guidebook* by Ralph Neighbour, and *Living Proof* by Jim Petersen. Realize that the curriculum isn't the biggest factor, though. The real issue is asking God to give you a new heart and a new lifestyle.

### Design it.

Have you designed a plan for equipping your church in relational outreach? If not, how are you going to do it? We are encouraged in 1 Peter 3:15 to "always be prepared to give the reason for the hope that you have. But do this with gentleness and respect." Do people know how to share their testimony and a simple presentation of the gospel? Do they know how to be sensitive to people and to the Holy Spirit so that it is done in a caring, respectful way? Are they forming friendships with unbelievers, so that people even ask about the hope within your cell members' lives?

Once the leadership begins to live relational outreach, the next step is to design a plan to equip as many as possible. You will often need two plans, one for the transition phase where you are shaping new values and another for equipping people within the emerging cell system once it is established.

### Discern it.

Listen to God. What specific plans does He have for you as a church? Is there a certain target group that he is calling you to target such as singles, young families or a particular ethnic group? Are there harvest events that He wants you to try? Pray! Consider fasting. What is God saying to you as you submit to him? The goal is not to get God running with your plan, but to get yourself running with God's plan!

As you move forward in outreach, understand that the cell system is like an extension cord. It has no power in and of itself. But if you plug it into God on one end and unbelievers on the other, life changing power can flow. Put the pieces of your cell strategy in place. That's essential. But even more essential is to plug it in. Connect to God and to the hurting world around you, then let

Christ's life and power flow through you. Jesus has made His intentions clear: "Remain in me, and I will remain in you. . . . This is to my Father's glory, that you bear much fruit showing yourselves to be my disciples" (John 15:4,8)

# 36

## The Empty Chair

by Ralph W. Neighbour, Jr.

An empty chair for a special person can significantly impact a cell meeting. Many cell leaders use an empty chair during times of sharing vision. The chair helps cell members to focus on unbelievers whose hearts need to be opened. The names of unbelievers can be written on slips of paper and placed on the seat of the chair, which becomes a focal point for intercession.

Cell members can be invited to sit in the empty chair and share their burden for an unsaved friend or relative. After the burdens are shared as person after person sits in the chair, cell members can surround the chair and pray for all those who were mentioned.

### The Holy Spirit's Chair.

In most Korean churches, there is a special chair on the platform for the Holy Spirit. The senior pastor sits on the right of it, others sit on the left. Often there is a golden pillow placed on its seat. Sometimes it is larger than the other chairs or elevated on a small platform. A sense of God's presence is symbolized as the people meet for worship and prayer.

The same impact can be had in a cell. Whenever you celebrate the Lord's Supper in your cell, place an empty chair at the table for the Holy Spirit. At the beginning of the meal, you might sing the chorus, "Holy Spirit, You are Welcome in this Place." The presence of the chair will significantly influence the time spent around the table.

**Chair for the Hurting.**

Bill and Betty had a group for parents of retarded children. Sometimes the pain in these parents was so great they could not share with the group. A white velvet chair in the living room was designated as the "silent chair." Any member who sat in it was treated with gentleness and special love. Thus, they could be nurtured within the cell without feeling guilty that they could not help others. This empty chair became very important to the group. Try this if you have a group where one or more people are going through a crisis, or experiencing deep emotional pain.

Be creative with this idea. Think about other ways an empty chair can symbolize important spiritual concepts. Implement them in your cell.

# 37

# Make Your Cell Meeting Visitor-Friendly
by Jim Egli

Ellen came to my cell group the first time with her neighbor, one of our cell members. She was an older woman who was recently divorced. While she came with mixed feelings, she was hungry for God and glad for the invitation. She trusted the new friends who had invited her, but she had never heard of a cell group. "Perhaps this was some kind of cult!" Ellen thought.

Cell members greeted her warmly when she arrived at our home and took a genuine interest in her. The songs were new, but there were song sheets and she liked their lively tempo. Later in the meeting, however, she was puzzled when I announced that we would "prayerwalk" the neighborhood. I didn't realize how this would come across and didn't notice that she was uncomfortable. Thankfully, Ken — an alert cell member — noticed her discomfort and remained at the house and spoke with her about recent changes that had taken place in her life while the rest of us walked around the neighborhood praying.

When the meeting was over, she enjoyed talking with others over refreshments. She left thinking that this would be a nice group of people to have as friends and that they didn't seem to be a cult. She was unsure, however, if she would come back. Did people like her? Would they be glad for her to return? My wife and another cell member called her on the phone that week, and her friends invited her back. She became actively involved in the group and began to receive healing for the past and support for the future.

Through my years in cell, I have learned a few simple things that make a big difference in making visitors feel more comfortable when they come to your cell. Here they are:

- Introduce your non-Christian and new Christian friends to as many cell members as possible. Do this through meals, parties and other shared events. The more cell members a person knows, the easier it is for them to visit a cell.

- Have the meeting at the home of the member who has invited someone new. When a member has a friend who is open to visiting your cell meeting, consider having the meeting at that cell member's home next week or even for several weeks. It's much easier for your friend to come to your home than to go with you to someone else's house (unless, the visitor has been introduced to that friend outside of a cell meeting.)

- Use an easy, "history" type of icebreaker. This is not the week to ask more probing questions like, "What stronghold do want to be delivered from this year?" A better icebreaker would be a Quaker Question like, "Where did you live between the ages of 7 and 12 years?"

- Use song sheets and sing fewer songs. New Christians and non-Christians do not know your songs. Since worship is usually near the front of the meeting, extended singing can seem awkward to them.

- As you begin the meeting, explain the purpose of a cell group. "We meet to experience the presence, power and purpose of Jesus!" Explain other things as the meeting proceeds that might be taken for granted, i.e., what the children are going to do when someone takes them into another room.

- Do not go around the circle asking people to read. They may not have a Bible, may not know where to find the book of James if they have one and may have limited reading skills that embarrass them.

- End on time! This means keeping each part of the meeting on track. When you end on time, there is time for the very important fellowship afterward.

- Follow-up on newcomers. Be sure to call them and drop them a note, expressing appreciation for their visit . . . and invite them back!

Loving non-Christians to Christ involves praying for them, caring about them, being their friend and letting them serve you. They need God, friends and relationships. The perfect place for them to find what they need is in your cell. When they show up, welcome them, be considerate of their needs and let them know you're glad they came. Like Ellen, they will find a family where Christ can minister life, healing and belonging!

# ADDITIONAL TOUCH RESOURCES ON CELLS

### WHERE DO WE GO FROM HERE? 10th Anniversary Edition
*by Ralph W. Neighbour, Jr.*
With updated data on new cell church models, new information on equipping and harvest events and practical teaching on how to begin a transition, this book will continue to stir hearts to dream about what the church can be. You will find hope for the church in North America and discover the new things that Dr. Neighbour has learned over the last 10 years. Share this vision with a friend. 400 pgs.

### GROUPS OF 12 *by Joel Comiskey*
Finally, the definitive work that clears the confusion about the Groups of 12 model. Thousands of pastors have traveled to International Charismatic Mission to see it in operation. In this new title, Joel has dug deeply into ICM and other G-12 churches to learn the simple G-12 principles that can be transferred to your church. This book will contrast this new model from the classic structure and show you exactly what to do with this new model of cell ministry. 182 pgs.

### REAP THE HARVEST *by Joel Comiskey*
This book will help you become more effective as you recognize missing components in your system, develop a blueprint for getting on the right track if you're struggling with a transition to cells and start over if you've failed and want to rebuild your cell structure with healthy cells that multiply. 240 pgs.

### UPWARD, INWARD, OUTWARD, FORWARD *by Jim Egli*
This workbook will help you prioritize key elements of small group life that will result in personal growth for yourself and each of your group members. The unique planning time, mixed with practical instruction will show you how to "put feet" on the ministry of Jesus in your group. When you implement the ideas, methods and events found here, your group will grow. We guarantee it! 72 pgs.

### CellGroup JOURNAL
*CellGroup Journal*, unlike any other periodical, is focused on the needs and desires of cell leaders in your church. Every quarterly issue contains practical feature articles and columns from some of the most respected leaders in the US including Ralph W. Neighbour, Jr., Billy Hornsby on leadership, Karen Hurston on evangelism, Gerrit Gustafson on worship, Sam Scaggs on missions, and Larry Kreider with a closing note on a variety of topics. Pastor's get fed too . . . each issue contains an article for pastors by a pastor who has learned a good lesson in cell life and wants to share. Bulk discounts are available for larger subscriptions.
Call today to subscribe for all your cell leaders and staff!

## ORDER TOLL-FREE! 1-800-735-5865
Order Online: www.touchusa.org

# ENCOUNTER GOD
## A PRACTICAL RESOURCE TO SET YOUR CHURCH FREE!

Growing churches around the world are using "encuentro, spiritual victory or deliverance weekends" to set their people free for ministry. Now you can too.

This user-friendly material has been tested in churches across North America and it works! This complete package will not only show you how to lead an *Encounter God Retreat*, the videos can actually facilitate the retreat for you.

Includes:

***Instructor's Guide:*** These teaching outlines explain the objectives and demonstrate how to teach every session of the weekend. Contains passwords to download presentations from our website. **SKU# EG2**

***Participants Manual:*** Each retreat participant receives a manual, which will not only help them learn about freedom in Christ, it will show them how to experience it. **SKU# EG1**

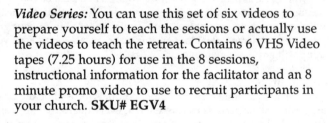

***Video Series:*** You can use this set of six videos to prepare yourself to teach the sessions or actually use the videos to teach the retreat. Contains 6 VHS Video tapes (7.25 hours) for use in the 8 sessions, instructional information for the facilitator and an 8 minute promo video to use to recruit participants in your church. **SKU# EGV4**

***Retreat Guide:*** This booklet will show you how to organize an *Encounter God Retreat*, explaining what to do and what to avoid. It also gives scheduling options for your retreat. **SKU# EG3**

Purchase all four items and save! **SKU# EGB5**

## ORDER TOLL-FREE! 1-800-735-5865
Order Online: www.touchusa.org